THE PATH
OF
PERFECTION

BAHRAM ELAHI, M.D.

Library of Congress Control Number: 2005905802

ISBN: 0-9764986-0-X

First Paraview, Inc. trade paperback edition March 2005

English translation by Monica Stevens and Michael Miller

Manufactured in the United States of America

CONTENTS

Face-to-Face with our Destiny

Life in Society

SPIRITUAL COMMUNICATION

THE PATH OF PERFECTION

APPENDIX

Fundamental Principles

1. THE MEANING OF LIFE

Once we understand where we have come from,
why we are here, and where we are going, we will
realize what we must do; from then on, we will
no longer remain in a state of confusion.[1]

Life is meaningful, and existence is not without purpose. We are neither created by chance, nor will we return to nothingness. We are not merely a biological body, and the specificity of our consciousness is such that it cannot simply be the product of the biochemical reactions of neurons. Although our biological organism or body is itself a marvel of creation, there is something more to the true nature of human beings: in reality, each of us is a celestial organism that has been merged with a terrestrial psyche to form a *psychospiritual organism*.

If we are essentially a celestial organism, why are we in this world and where are we headed? Once we find the answers to these questions, our suffering will subside, our sense of obscurity will disappear, and we will discover the meaning of life.

The Universe is Meaningful

Every particle in the universe has "life," for it is in constant motion and evolution. Everything exists for a reason and a purpose, and each particle, even the most insignificant, has a given source, a designated function, and a specific destination. At the origin and heart of the perceptible and imperceptible world, there is an extremely powerful, intelligent, willful, active, and benevolent thought that encompasses and governs all things. What we call it—Creator, Yahweh, God, Allah, Truth, Total Being—is of no significance; what is important is to know that it is this unique Source that the founders of the great monotheistic faiths have recognized, and it is His traces that researchers in the experimental sciences have observed in the mechanisms governing living organisms and the world of particles, without necessarily recognizing Him. All that exists originates from this Source and, after completing its necessary growth (its process of perfection), will return to Him.

We are able to directly observe the ultimate maturation of living organisms such as plants and animals. For example, fruit is the culmination of the natural growth (perfection) of a bud. In human beings, a fetus evolves into a newborn, then an adolescent, and ultimately into a mature adult. Parallel to the process of physical development, there is also a **process of spiritual perfection** for all beings. The energy for this process of spiritual perfection derives from an ascending "gravitational" force that engenders in all beings an inner movement called the *transubstantial movement,* whose direction is always geared toward the Source. In human beings, however, in addition to this general and automatic transubstantial movement, there also exists a specific, conscious, and voluntary movement toward spiritual perfection whose direction is subject to each individual's free will and willpower.

What is a Human Being?

In the terrestrial world, humans are two-dimensional beings composed of a body and a soul. The biological body is a temporary receptacle (mold) for the **celestial soul** and, at the same time, a necessary complement for the process of spiritual perfection of the "**self**" or psychospiritual organism. In essence, human beings are composed of the celestial soul, which constitutes their true identity and survives the death of the physical body. Therefore, we can say that we are essentially a psychospiritual organism in the mold of a body.

The self or psychospiritual organism, however, is not an abstract entity devoid of individuality, but rather a "material" being, though

18

of such subtle matter that the sensory organs of the body are normally unable to perceive it.[2] This organism is the source of our self-consciousness, perceptions, feelings, and other aptitudes considered to be part of the specificity of human beings. The self is endowed with the potential to develop and evolve toward its maturity (perfection), and whenever this potential is fully realized, we have reached the ultimate stage of our spiritual growth, meaning perfection.

In summary, a human being or the self is essentially a psychospiritual organism temporarily residing in a biological body. What endows a human being with an identity, what engenders thought within him and causes him to feel that he exists and will continue to exist after death is this psychospiritual organism or self.

The Process of Perfection of the "Self"

Like other responsible beings in the universe, human beings must undertake their own process of spiritual perfection, a task for which they bear direct responsibility. The path of perfection is a process of reaching maturation or spiritual perfection and consists of numerous stages. Aside from exceptional cases, a single terrestrial life is usually insufficient to complete all of these stages.

In the material world, our process of perfection consists in gradually developing virtues within ourselves that we call *divine virtues* (such as compassion, generosity, rectitude, etc.). A divine virtue is a balanced and perfect attribute that becomes part of one's nature and of the same quality as His attributes. From its inception, each divine virtue acts as a source of light that shines in the unconscious of an individual and illuminates his mind. Acquiring even a single divine virtue is like a permanent source of bliss that one constantly feels and from which others benefit as well. The perfection of a human being occurs when he reaches the ultimate level of psychospiritual maturity—that is, when he succeeds in cultivating the totality of divine virtues within himself to the extent of his abilities and makes them part of his nature. That is when an individual unites with the Source, experiences absolute freedom, and becomes eternal in a state of ineffable bliss while preserving his own identity.

Why Are We Here?

The purpose of our presence on earth is to undergo the embryonic stage of the celestial soul's development. Just as the biological embryo needs the maternal womb for its growth and development, the psychospiritual organism or self also needs a suitable environment (earthly life) for its growth and perfection. During the soul's embryonic stage, the psychospiritual organism acquires from earthly life the basic elements necessary for its development via the psyche. It is therefore essential to undergo the stage of terrestrial life in order to lay the foundations of our spiritual perfection.

What Should We Do?

The natural development of the soul requires sufficient knowledge of the **causal** principles that govern the spiritual domain.[3] This means that just as protecting one's health and ensuring the proper development of the body (biological organism) requires knowledge of the causal principles that govern the body's health (the science of medicine provides us with access to such principles), preserving the health of the self (psychospiritual organism) requires knowledge of the causal principles that govern the self. This knowledge constitutes the science that we call *natural spirituality* or *medicine of the soul*.[4] As such, it is only by respecting the spiritual principles that govern the celestial soul that we can ensure the health and development of the self in accordance with its nature.

2. A Few Basic Axioms

By virtue of divine grace, all beings will eventually arrive at perfection and will benefit from divine justice, except those who have incurred the divine wrath …

Every science is based on a set of axioms and basic concepts.[1] For example, a "point" is a fundamental concept of geometry. Despite the fact that the existence of a point has not been proven, we can observe its effects at all levels, from mathematical constructions to architectural designs. Similarly, if we consider the process of spiritual perfection as a science, it too must be based on a number of fundamental axioms and concepts. In this science, for instance, the *divine presence* in every point of the universe can be considered as one of the axioms of the process of spiritual perfection. Just as a point is present in every geometrical form and structure despite being invisible, the divine presence, normally imperceptible to our five physical senses, is present in every element of creation as well.

Divine Presence

The first basic axiom in the science of spiritual perfection is the divine presence. Although it is possible to become aware of this presence, it cannot be conveyed or proven to those who have yet to internally realize the faculty of detecting this presence. Human beings have been endowed with the potential to become aware of and to perceive this presence, but the awakening of this faculty is completely dependent upon the level of development the celestial soul has attained through a correct education of thought. If our thought remains uneducated or is incorrectly educated, the potential to perceive this presence may fade and not be realized, in which case no argument will be able to convince us of this presence.

Many of those who deny the Source are in fact rejecting the image of Him that has been created in their minds based on the dogmatic imaginations and terrestrial desires of others.[2] If He were described the way He truly is and not according to manmade conceptions and interests, everyone would have faith in Him. The true Source is such that if we were to perceive even a pale reflection of His manifestation, no one would be able not to have faith in Him with certitude and not to be overwhelmed by his kindness.

Whoever sees a manifestation of the Source or feels His presence cannot resist His captivating love; many have attested to this. His manifestation is a radiance of ineffable power that is at the same time very delicate, delightful, and deeply reassuring such that it completely encompasses us. We feel His presence everywhere and in everything: within us and outside of us, everywhere we look it is He. His presence is perceived as an intelligent and extremely powerful energy, overflowing with ineffable affection, grandeur, clemency, justice, grace, forbearance, etc.

Causality

Another basic axiom in the science of spiritual perfection is the *principle of causality*. The existence of all beings, including the spiritual universe, is based on the principle of causality. Everything has a cause and a reason, and progress can only be achieved through the channels of causality. Everything that exists has come into existence from the cause or causes that preceded it, and in turn constitutes the cause or one of the causes for the subsequent beings that follow it. It is only the Creator—based on the dictates of reason—that is without cause and is Himself the creator of all causes.[3] He created the first being of the universe, or the First Cause, which in a sense is the "primordial substance" of all creation and the origin of the totality of material and spiritual worlds, as well as all possible and existent beings. Creation begins with the First Cause and then gradually continues from one cause to the next. The appearance of beings in all of creation thus takes place gradually through the chain of cause and effects that we call *the descending pathway*. Each species appears at a designated moment, remains for a determined period of time after which it becomes extinct, and is then followed by the appearance of other species.

Beings each undergo the descending pathway from one cause to the next until their point of appearance: they then begin an ascending movement of return toward the Source called *the process of spiritual perfection*. The process of spiritual perfection is the course that every being must follow to reach its maturation and perfection—a level of spiritual maturity, perception, and alertness that enables it to communicate with all beings and to fully benefit from all the graces of the universe.

Vital Essence

The third basic axiom in the science of spiritual perfection is the *vital essence*. The vital essence engenders life and transubstantial movement in beings. Accordingly, as a result of a continuous and evolving flux called the transubstantial movement, all beings are physically and spiritually moving toward their origin, meaning the Source. The energy necessary for this movement comes from that which we call life or the vital essence, and the source of this energy is none other than the Necessary Being.

In reality, the vital essence is the effect of the divine presence in beings: although we cannot see it, this essence exists in all beings and endows them with self-consciousness. As soon as the vital essence is separated from a being, it ceases to have any movement or life.

There are, of course, other axioms at work in creation, but based on the two axioms of causality and divine presence, we can deduce a few practical, spiritual rules. Considering that everything has a cause and that scientists are certain they can find answers to their questions by retracing the chains of causality, in the spiritual realm it is also possible to find answers to most questions about the spiritual world by relying on the principle of causality, with the difference that perceiving the causal levels of the spiritual world is not possible without receiving divine light, and it is only with the help of the axiom of divine presence that we can attract such light.

The other conclusion we can draw is that to reach any goal requires the use of causes and means that are suitable to that goal. For example, someone who wants to become a physician must learn the science of medicine. Likewise, if we want to reach spiritual perfection, we must learn the science of self-knowledge that culminates in divine knowledge, or else we may end up with an undesirable result.

3. THE PROCESS OF PERFECTION

> *The process of perfection from minerals to plants, plants to animals, and animals to humans is determined, whereas human beings are themselves responsible for choosing the right path as a result of their transcendent reason.*

Human beings, like all other beings in the material world, have the potential to grow, evolve, and reach perfection, although their process of perfection has its own specificity. To better understand the nature of this specificity, it is necessary to have an overview of the general process of perfection of beings on earth.

The invisible dimension of beings is what we call the *vital essence* or *soul*, while their visible dimension is called the body. "Inert" matter does not exist: the vital essence animates all beings with a continuous movement—called the transubstantial movement—as a result of which they advance toward perfection, continuously evolving and transforming along the way while preserving their individual identities. The general process of perfection of all beings, from the least complex, which are minerals, to the most complex, which on earth are human beings, takes place through this transubstantial movement.[1]

Up to the level of human beings, the vital essences (spirits) do not have any individuality. Like the water molecules of a river current that form a unified whole despite retaining their molecular identity, these vital essences bind with one another to form currents of mineral, vegetal, and animal spirits while retaining their individual identities. Following the necessary stages of accumulation, evolution, and transformations, the current of mineral spirits (the spiritual current within minerals), to which new vital essences are continuously added, graduates into the current of vegetal spirits and, in the same manner, the current of vegetal spirits transforms into the current of animal spirits....

In other words, after attaining perfection, the current of mineral spirits—the vital essence that exists in minerals—transforms into the current of vegetal spirits. The vegetal spirit is the vital essence that results in the development and growth of plants. For example, a seed deprived of its vegetal spirit is considered dead, for although it is outwardly indistinguishable from the other seeds, it lacks the potential to germinate and grow. In the mineral kingdom, this difference is apparent in certain precious stones that have lost their special luster (life): without their own specific mineral soul, such stones will gradually decompose.

In the same manner, the current of vegetal spirits will in turn reach perfection and transform into the current of animal spirits. This process of perfection continues until the current of animal spirits transforms into the current of the **terrestrial spirit**.[2] The terrestrial spirit (soul) is specific to human beings and constitutes the perfection of the animal spirit. Unlike the necessarily collective existence of spirits at the lower levels, the terrestrial spirit is an independent unit that possesses its own individual identity.

It is as a result of this accumulation and process of perfection, then, that a spirit is transformed into another spirit of a higher level. In each species, it is the spirit that evolves, not the body. The physical form of each species is the materialization of a spiritual archetype; in other words, the body is the materialization of a primordial spiritual archetype, which establishes the order of material elements and results in the establishment of the order and governance of beings.[3] It is the spirit that imparts life and form, contributing to the order and cohesion of a being's physical dimension. The complexity of each species corresponds to its degree of spiritual perfection.

Considering that the movement of the general process of perfection of beings is continuous, gradual, and ascending, each spirit carries within it the characteristics of the more primitive spirits that contributed to its formation, along with the germ of higher spirits.[4] For example, fertile soil bears certain elements of the vegetal spirit, or the terrestrial soul of human beings carries the imprints of mineral, vegetal, and animal spirits: the imprints of the mineral spirit, for instance, can be observed in the bones; the growth of hair and nails is indicative of the presence of the vegetal spirit; and the animal spirit is manifest in one's blood, instincts, desires, emotions, etc.

In the causal order of creation, matter is an indispensable receptacle for the soul, for it provides the soul with a means to take on a body and to consequently evolve toward its perfection. An animal therefore is a receptacle for the animal spirit, just as a plant is a receptacle for the vegetal spirit. Although the material receptacle breaks down after losing its spirit (i.e., physical death) and its constitutive elements once again form new structures, the soul continues its life and pursues its perfection in a higher spirit, without losing its identity.

4. The Process of Spiritual Perfection

The process of perfection of human beings is the process of perfection of the celestial soul.

Like all other perceptible beings, human beings possess a visible dimension (the body) and an invisible dimension (the soul). In their visible dimension, human beings are but a mammal from the order of primates, and like other primates, they have instincts, vital needs, emotions, etc., of an animal nature. Their invisible dimension, however, is exceptional because it is the result of the fusion of two souls—the terrestrial soul and the celestial soul—which form a *psychospiritual organism* that we call the "*self.*" The particular specificity of the self stems from having a celestial soul, whose existence is indicative of the clear difference between human consciousness and animal consciousness.

The terrestrial spirit, with its earthly origin, endows the body with life and ensures its biological existence;[1] this spirit corresponds to what is called the **id** in psychoanalysis, or the source of animalistic impulses. The terrestrial soul manifests itself in the human psyche in the form of instincts, desires, emotions (animalistic), etc. In the body, the terrestrial spirit expresses itself primarily through the autonomous nervous centers (the unconscious), whereas the celestial spirit expresses itself through the cerebral cortex (the center of consciousness). The autonomous nervous centers that ensure animal life are in constant interaction with the cerebral cortex.

The celestial spirit has a heavenly origin, and its presence can be observed in what psychoanalysis calls the **ego** and the **super-ego**. The celestial spirit comes directly from the divine Source, and manifests itself in the realm of the psyche through the conscious ego, reason, the voice of the conscience, creativity, faith, etc. The presence of the celestial spirit gives human beings the ability to oppose their terrestrial animal impulses when necessary, and even to completely control them at some point.

As a consequence of these graces bestowed upon human beings, their process of spiritual perfection is based on free will, unlike that of minerals, plants, and animals, which is determined and directed by nature. In other words, human beings are each responsible for their spiritual perfection, and must use their faculty of discernment and free will to choose a correct path. The faculty of free will given to human beings is an exceptional privilege, for it is only through such a conscious and willful process of perfection that human beings can reach total consciousness. Those who have surpassed the bounds of ordinary self-consciousness and have reached total consciousness are in a position to understand total bliss and peace.

From the moment of conception, the embryo receives its life from the terrestrial soul, whereas the celestial soul is usually insufflated into the newborn at the moment of birth, at which point the terrestrial and celestial souls merge together to form the self. As long as human beings live on earth, they are the seat of a constant inner struggle between the two parts of their self: on one side, reason and the voice of their conscience, which originate from the celestial soul, and on the other side, the animal impulses (instincts, natural needs, etc.) that originate from the terrestrial soul. The terrestrial soul draws us toward worldly pleasures, while the celestial soul, which bears the **divine particle**, draws us toward the divine Source. This constant confrontation between these opposing forces is what drives the spiritual process of perfection in human beings, and depending on which of the two forces dominates us, we can either actualize or waste the potential to perfect ourselves.

Although the terrestrial body decomposes[2] into its constitutive elements after death and returns to the earth, the terrestrial soul continues its life within the celestial soul, which is destined to remain alive eternally. Consequently, the process of perfection of human beings is the process of perfection of the celestial soul.

In some respects, the process of perfection of the psychospiritual organism or the self is analogous to the process of an infant's growth and development. At the time of birth, a newborn does not have a clear consciousness of his own being or his surrounding environment. Although his physical and mental potentials will gradually develop, it is only when they have reached a sufficient level of growth and maturity that he can have a clearer consciousness of his condition and surroundings, and benefit from his advantages. Likewise, although the spiritual dimension of human beings bears its own potentials and the faculty to attain spiritual consciousness, it is only when these spiritual potentials are realized and their spiritual consciousness reaches complete maturity (perfection) that they can attain a completely clear consciousness of themselves and the whole of creation, and fully benefit from all of its graces.

5. THE SELF, THE TOTAL EGO
(PART I - THE CELESTIAL COMPONENT)

If the celestial soul is covered with black smoke arising from the desires and whims of the imperious self, the radiance of its divine particle will no longer be visible.

Through their own choices, human beings can determine the direction of their spiritual development. To understand this specificity, we have to simultaneously consider human beings in their psychological and spiritual dimensions. Such an approach provides for a new definition of the human personality or "self" that is more comprehensive than that which is found in psychoanalysis. We will nonetheless begin with some of the contributions and fundamental concepts in psychoanalysis to better clarify the concept of the self.

The Human Personality or "Self" According to Psychoanalysis
From the viewpoint of psychoanalysis, the three basic components of the human personality or self can be summarized as the *id*, the *ego*, and the *superego*, each of which is situated in three levels of an individual's consciousness: the *conscious*, the *preconscious*, and the *unconscious*.[1] Only a small part of the ego and the superego are located within the conscious; the remainder lies in the preconscious and the unconscious.

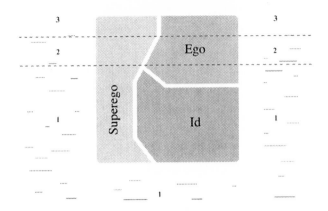

[Figure 1]
The psychological structure of human beings according to psychoanalysis
1. The Unconscious 2. The Preconscious 3. The Conscious

♦ According to psychoanalysis, the id, generally situated in the unconscious, is the source of our biological impulses, instincts, vital needs, aggressive tendencies, etc. Subject entirely to the pleasure principle, the id acts like a child or animal that is neither mindful of realities nor concerned with ethics or reason. It is incapable of anything except wanting and acting upon its instincts.

♦ The ego is the seat of reason and the source of thought. Its function is to regulate the conflicts and struggles that arise between the impulses of the id, on the one hand, and the prohibitions of the superego (the moral conscience), on the other. Developing gradually through contact with its environment, the ego is governed by the principle of realism, which leads it to evaluate the reality and consequences of actions resulting from the needs of the id.

♦ The superego is the source of the moral conscience, and its function is to discern the good and evil of every action the ego performs under the influence of the impulses of the id.

The superego develops through contact with the social environment and its moral prohibitions, and is the origin of the voice of our conscience, the sense of remorse, and the feeling of guilt.

These three structures of a human being's psychological personality are in constant conflict, and the manner in which these conflicts are resolved determines an individual's behavior.

The self as described and explained by psychoanalysis limits the human personality to its terrestrial dimension without generally considering or recognizing its celestial dimension. If the self is limited solely to the terrestrial dimension, however, how can we explain certain behaviors that transcend human nature? For example, how can we ignore the existence of a transcendent force that leads some to prefer death over disgrace and shame, in spite of their instinct of self-preservation? What is the transcendent force that allows one to overcome the desires of the id or of one's nature, desires that appear logical according to the ego's judgment but contrary to one's moral conscience or divine satisfaction? The answer lies in the celestial soul, which is the source of such transcendent behaviors in human beings. Animals, even those that are closest to us from a biological standpoint, are incapable of transcendent behavior—for example, acting upon the voice of their conscience— for moral consciousness has a celestial origin and animals are devoid of a celestial soul. Therefore, we are led to consider a more comprehensive definition of the self that also takes into account the celestial dimension of the human personality, one which we call the **total ego.**

The Human Personality According to the Concept of the Total Ego

The total ego or the real self (*Figure 2*) differs from the self described by psychoanalysis in four essential respects:

1) the presence of the celestial soul;

2) the ego is not limited solely to that of our present psyche, but also includes all of the egos from our past lives;

3) the superego is not merely confined to our moral or **blaming conscience**, but also includes two other consciences—the **inspiring conscience** and the **certifying conscience**;

4) the addition of a fourth component—the **super id**, which is the origin of spiritual impulses—to the three basic components of the human personality: the ego, the superego, and the id (See Chapter 38).

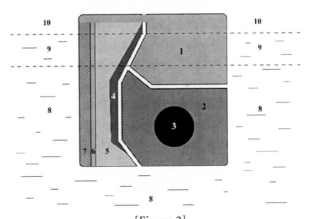

[Figure 2]

The psychospiritual structure of human beings according to the concept of the Total Ego

1. The Ego
2. The Id
3. The Imperious Self
4. The Super Id
5. The Blaming Conscience
6. The Inspiring Conscience ── Superego
7. The Certifying Conscience

8. The Unconscious
9. The Preconscious
10. The Conscious

Celestial Soul: Ego, Superego (blaming conscience, inspiring conscience, certifying conscience), Super Id.

Terrestrial Soul or Id (Worker Self – Imperious Self)

1) The Celestial Soul

The celestial soul bears a particle that originates from the breath of the divine soul and confers upon human beings the potential to develop divine virtues. Although the celestial soul is initially created "pure" and endowed with a tremendous potential for development, it is immature and thus like a child that is still incapable of discerning between good and evil. To evolve, the celestial soul must merge with its complement, the terrestrial soul. Due to its origin and nature, the celestial soul is attracted toward the Source and benevolence, and is devoid of any negative attributes (pride, rancor, jealousy, etc.), whereas the terrestrial soul, on account of its origin and nature, bears the opposite tendencies. It is this opposition that enables the celestial soul to realize its potential for growth and development.

Diversity is required for creation to be complete. Celestial souls, therefore, do not all belong to the same group, and are endowed with various capacities and levels, which partially explains the diversity in human psyches. Celestial souls can be analogized to containers with capacities ranging from a few drops of water to an entire sea or even more. Divine justice, however, prevents individuals with celestial souls that are endowed with a greater creational capacity to work less in order to gain proximity to the Source. That is why at the outset the ability of the celestial soul to control the terrestrial soul is counterbalanced by the power of the attacks of the **imperious self**.[2] Consequently, at the beginning of the path, the balance of power between the ego and the id (the celestial soul and the terrestrial soul) is the same for everyone.

Whether the capacity of a celestial soul is equivalent to a drop of water or an entire sea, once it reaches perfection it enters the divine ocean. Thus, regardless of the celestial soul's initial capacity, whoever reaches total inner equilibrium—meaning spiritual perfection—attains total happiness, feels absolute bliss, and no longer desires anything more than what he is. Of course, the level or rank one occupies in the spiritual world is contingent upon the amount of divine light one has absorbed. In general, however, the spiritual rank of perfect spirits that occupy the lowest levels of the world of perfection is infinitely superior to that of other beings, even those who reside in the highest levels of eternal paradise.[3] According to the definition of the self presented here, apart from the id, the other components—namely, the ego, the superego, and the super id—belong to the celestial soul.

2) The Ego

The ego is synonymous with our own self. It is the source of our intelligence, reason, reflection, the faculty of discernment, willpower, creativity, and our other senses. All our perceptions, each and every one of our voluntary decisions, and all of our thoughts, reasoning, intentions, etc., stem from the ego. It is responsible for imposing its will on all the other components of the self, especially the imperious self. The ego is constantly interacting with the brain, through which it transmits its commands to all parts of the self. Like the other components of the celestial soul, the ego remains after the brain perishes.

3) The Superego

The superego is composed of three faculties or consciences, which serve as the tools of the ego. Through these three faculties—the blaming conscience, the inspiring conscience, and the certifying conscience—the celestial soul makes itself heard by the conscious self.

When someone acts contrary to his conscience or has an incorrect intention, the blaming or moral conscience reproaches him. If the energy of the blaming conscience exceeds a certain limit, it will engender an inner feeling of pathological guilt; on the other hand, if the energy from this faculty is below a certain level, it will transform an individual into a dangerous monster capable of committing evil without any remorse. Once the energy from this faculty is in equilibrium, however, an individual becomes conscionable, equitable, righteous, etc. As for the certifying conscience, whenever we perform a positive act with a moral or divine intention, we experience a feeling of joy and contentment that confirms the correctness of our act—this feeling stems from the effect of the certifying conscience, while the inspiring conscience provides us with inspiration as to what is good and bad.

4) The Super Id

In contrast to the id, which is the source of natural or biological impulses, the super id is the source of our metaphysical impulses, which can be spiritually divine like those of the truly detached mystics of the past, or non-divine or even anti-divine, such as the motivation to perform paranormal phenomena.[4] The natural attraction of the majority of human beings toward spirituality and the Source stems from the super id, which is why this attraction is irrepressible. If the impulses of the super id are frustrated, repressed, or uncontrolled by a prudent ego, they may lead to various psychospiritual functional impairments as in the case of the id. For example, if mystical impulses are not controlled by a prudent ego, they may result in psychological and spiritual ruin.

6. THE SELF, THE TOTAL EGO
(PART II - THE TERRESTRIAL COMPONENT)

Beware that the imperious self does not govern you.

The terrestrial soul, which constitutes a structural component of the "self" or the total ego, closely corresponds to the concept of the id in psychoanalysis, and is the source of the impulsive, instinctive, and emotional behaviors of the self, as well as the natural needs of the body. Similar to the id, the terrestrial soul does not recognize morals, religion, law, etc., and thus ignores all social, familial, and ethical conventions. Its behavior is like that of a small child or animal that seeks to instantly satisfy its desires in a purely selfish manner.

The terrestrial soul (id) is composed of three faculties or components: the **concupiscent faculty**, the **irascible faculty**, and the **imaginative faculty**.

♦ The concupiscent faculty produces the necessary psychological energy for impulses geared toward desire and pleasure. An excess of this energy engenders hedonism, greed, jealousy, etc., whereas a deficiency of such energy results in depression, a kind of pessimism, and so forth. Once this faculty is in equilibrium, however, it will generate modesty, self-restraint, and temperance, ensuring preservation of the self and the species.

♦ The irascible faculty produces the necessary psychological energy for the fight-or-flight response. In excess, the irascible faculty engenders wrath, aggression, violence, oppression, etc., whereas a deficiency of such energy results in lethargy, a lack of zeal, a lack of effort, a lack of self-esteem, etc. In equilibrium, the irascible faculty engenders bravery and courage, as a result of which we can stand up to transgressions and defend our rights.

♦ The imaginative faculty creates awareness of details and is the source of imaginations, fantasies, etc.; it can be considered the intelligence of the terrestrial soul. If the energy of the imaginative faculty dominates the energy of the **transcendent reason**, it will result in trickery, hypocrisy, improbity, deception, reverie, etc.[1] On the other hand, if the energy from this faculty is deficient, it will lead to a lack of sound judgment, naiveté, foolishness, a lack of imagination, etc. When the energy of the imaginative faculty is combined with the energy of the transcendent reason in equilibrium, it engenders meticulousness, skillfulness, sagacity, tactfulness, prudence, etc.

These three faculties do not manifest in a pure state within human beings, but rather are in a constant state of interaction with one another and result in a variety of behavioral traits among human beings.

While the terrestrial soul is the source of our physical energy, it also provides part of our mental energy, which is why we must strictly avoid anything that threatens the health of our body, such as asceticism, drugs, or other substances that are toxic and harmful for the body and the mind (the psyche). If the body is weakened, the terrestrial soul is no longer able to produce the energy required for essential impulses—impulses that are necessary to sustain life and contribute to the process of spiritual perfection.

On the other hand, repressing certain tendencies of the terrestrial soul can aggravate other tendencies or create a psychological complex. For example, if someone represses his sexual instincts through physical asceticism or certain meditative techniques with the goal of acquiring supernatural powers, his natural tendencies will be suppressed and will create a complex with unimaginable pressure, such that when confronted with the first serious temptation, these tendencies will rebel and overtake control of his reason.

The terrestrial soul and its three faculties manifest themselves in the realm of the conscious as an entity with a double personality: one that is obedient and diligent, and one that is disobedient and deviant; we call the former the **worker self**[2] and the latter the **imperious self**.[3]

♦ In the form of the worker self, the terrestrial soul appears as a responsible and diligent worker that automatically and in accordance with its natural instincts regulates the biological and psychological functions of the body such as nutrition, reproduction, immunity, emotions, etc.

♦ In the form of the imperious self, the terrestrial soul appears as a capricious, disobedient, rebellious, aggressive, greedy, and deceptive being, seeking only to imperiously satisfy its whimsical desires, which are always illegitimate.

The imperious self does not have a creational existence per se, and essentially results from the temperament of noxious animals in the terrestrial soul; in other words, it is a state that derives from the dysfunction—an excess or deficiency—of the irascible, concupiscent, and imaginative faculties. These inner imbalances are expressed in the form of imperious impulses (the imperious self) within us. The imperious self can thus be considered as a rebellious agent of illegitimate and destructive desires of the terrestrial soul or id. When left uncontrolled by the ego, these destructive and harmful impulses will engender ethical faults and weak points as well as negative thoughts and feelings, and will drive human beings toward a loss of inner equilibrium and a lack of self-control.

In summary, the "true self" or "total ego" of human beings is a combination of the celestial soul, which originates from the divine

Source, and the terrestrial soul, which arises from nature. The celestial soul is similar to a guiding light, without which a human being is just another mammal among the higher primates, in which case his psyche is reduced to the level of the id. On the other hand, without the terrestrial soul a human being is merely an angel-like being, credulous and naive, unable to discern between good and evil. The terrestrial soul is therefore an essential complement for the celestial soul, which draws all the qualities required for its evolution from the terrestrial soul and uses the biological body as a working tool in the material world.

7. Controlling the "Self"

The "self" is inseparable from the celestial soul.

The "self" or the total ego is a living and dynamic psycho-spiritual organism that must grow and develop in its own suitable environment. Toward this end, its celestial part must draw the necessary "spiritual nutrients" for its growth, or what we call spiritual maturity, from the terrestrial part. The appropriate and balanced process of exchanges between these two parts of the self does not occur automatically, however, and requires the conscious and voluntary intervention of the ego to establish balanced exchanges between the two. Therefore, to understand a few basic concepts about the mechanism of this process, we need to first know how to positively intervene in the exchanges between these two parts of the self.

At the outset of its creation, the celestial soul can be likened to limpid water. Just as water is formed of molecular units, the celestial soul is formed of units called celestial **character units** from which the soul derives its specificities. In contrast, the terrestrial soul can be likened to an extremely concentrated solution consisting of character units or varied *terrestrial particles* that form the instincts, natural needs, and other tendencies of the terrestrial soul (id).

As soon as the two souls (celestial and terrestrial) merge to form the self, a constant power struggle between the two is ignited. If the celestial soul is healthy, from adolescence onward this struggle will manifest itself at the level of our conscious through an inner conflict. Each time we want to make a decision in daily life or are faced with situations involving emotions, faith, ethics, etc., we feel this inner struggle. The process of perfection, then, consists precisely in establishing equilibrium in the exchanges between these two conflicting parts of the self.

The manner of exchanges between these two parts occurs as if they were separated from one another by a selective osmotic membrane.[1] On one side of this membrane is the celestial soul ("limpid water"), and on the other side is the terrestrial soul (an extremely concentrated solution of terrestrial particles). Based on the law of osmosis, the passage of particles from the terrestrial soul to the celestial soul is automatic, meaning that if the ego remains passive and does not actively interfere in these exchanges, an excess of terrestrial particles will automatically enter the celestial soul and damage it. Conversely, if the ego is overly restrictive in the passage of these terrestrial particles and does not allow a sufficient number to pass through, it will slow the normal development of the celestial soul. For example, if an excess of particles from the imaginative faculty enter the celestial soul, they will result in a tendency toward trickery, conspiracy, reverie, etc., whereas a deficiency of such particles will lead to naiveté, credulity, etc.; in equilibrium, however, such particles will engender ingenuity and cleverness. Likewise, between the extremes of temerity and cowardice lies the attribute of courage, which is necessary for self-preservation and can result only if the necessary terrestrial particles enter the celestial soul in a sufficient amount.

The perfection of each attribute lies in its equilibrium, meaning in the proper amounts of its constitutive parts. Consequently, the ego's task of filtering terrestrial particles must be undertaken actively and in a balanced manner. In practice, filtering what passes through the membrane means controlling the harmful and illegitimate impulses of the terrestrial soul (the imperious self) through the help of one's willpower. Let us take the example of anger, for instance. Imagine that we find ourselves in a situation where our anger has been aroused. If we do not control this emotion, terrestrial particles of anger that have been released in excess will automatically enter our celestial soul and gradually damage its nature. But if we are able to control our anger, the appropriate amount of anger particles necessary for controlling the imperious self will enter the celestial soul. It is in such situations that we can voluntarily control the exchanges between the terrestrial and celestial parts and have a favorable effect on the structural composition of the self. In each given situation, the amount and kind of terrestrial particles that have to pass through the membrane depend on the extent to which we are in control of, or surrendered to, the illegitimate desires of the terrestrial soul (imperious self).

It is important to note that by imposing harsh ascetic regimens on the body or by practicing certain mental techniques such as meditation, it is possible to stop the production of some terrestrial particles—for example, the particles of sexual desires—or even to temporarily dry up such particles at their source. Such an approach, however, is harmful to the natural development of the self, for in such a state the amount of terrestrial particles necessary for completing the character units of the celestial soul will be insufficient. Thus, controlling the impulses of the terrestrial soul to acquire control over the imperious self does not mean weakening the body through difficult ascetic practices to the extent that we dry up the source of any such desire. The body, and the terrestrial spirit that gives it life, is a necessary mount for the celestial soul. The principles of natural spirituality require that this mount be strong but tame. Therefore, caring for the health of the body and providing it with its legitimate needs to the extent that it can fulfill its natural duties is an extremely important task. In other words, we must use all available means to preserve the health of the body and to establish equilibrium between body and soul.

If an individual does not actively struggle to establish equilibrium within his self, or remains ignorant or negligent, the imperious self will inevitably dominate his being and ultimately overtake his willpower. To avoid such a disaster, one must be vigilant and take control of the regulation of exchanges between one's celestial and terrestrial parts. If terrestrial particles enter the "limpid water" of the celestial soul in sufficient amounts, they will complete the celestial character units and engender within them the potential to evolve toward their perfection—that is, the potential to transform into divine virtues. Once all the character units of the celestial soul, with the help of the complementary particles from the terrestrial soul, have transformed into divine virtues, the self not only regains its initial transparency but also achieves perfect equilibrium and maximum lucidity. It is then that the attributes of the celestial soul acquire the qualities of divine attributes, i.e., perfection.

8. Celestial Reason

Only celestial reason can establish equilibrium between the four pillars of human life: body and soul, this world and the next.

Transcendent reason is part of the celestial soul and is the innate faculty of reasoning in the ego that enables human beings to manage their internal conflicts and to regulate the osmotic exchanges between their celestial and terrestrial parts. Transcendent reason cannot fulfill its duties completely and perfectly unless it is transformed into **celestial reason**.

Terrestrial Intellect and Celestial Reason

Terrestrial intellect is a state of the transcendent reason in which reason is subjugated to the imperious self. If we are not progressing in a correct spiritual direction, if we do not take any steps toward our spirituality, or if we remain indifferent or ignorant about our spiritual destiny and spend our time solely on material affairs, our transcendent reason will gradually be reduced to a terrestrial (animal) intellect. In such a state, the celestial soul becomes increasingly tarnished each day as a result of the successive attacks of the imperious self, and we become transformed into a selfish individual who is indifferent toward others. Our behavior then is completely animal-like due to the domination of the terrestrial intellect, as we are drawn only toward the attractions and pleasures of the terrestrial world and become heedless toward divine truths, viewing ethical and divine principles as outdated and futile. This downward spiral can continue to the extent that an individual knowingly and intentionally commits vile and animal-like acts not only without remorse, but with a sense of proud accomplishment as well.

Celestial reason, which is the source of prudence and temperance, constitutes the mature state of transcendent reason. The more transcendent reason is nourished with correct divine principles, the more it evolves in the direction of celestial reason, for a more balanced exchange occurs between the celestial and terrestrial parts of the self.[1] The more balanced these exchanges, the more harmonious and proportional the development of the self. As transcendent reason gradually evolves toward its celestial state, greater equilibrium is established between the four pillars of life—the soul and the body, this world and the next. Consequently, human virtues such as dutifulness, compassion, generosity, nobility, rectitude, dignity, forbearance, etc., are further developed in human beings.

The Evolution of Transcendent Reason

Transcendent reason is an innate part of the celestial soul that normally fluctuates on the spectrum between terrestrial intellect and celestial reason; the more it develops, the closer it draws to its celestial state. The extent of the evolution of transcendent reason into celestial reason can be measured by the intensity of an individual's inclination toward ethical and divine virtues, as well as the extent to which his celestial soul's character units have transformed into divine virtues. The more this intensity and transformation increases in an individual, the less likely it becomes that the imperious self will dominate him, the more correct his decisions become, and the closer his behavior comes to equilibrium. It all depends on the kinds of choices an individual makes: if he considers being attentive to the desires of the celestial soul as one of his essential duties and his actions are in accord with a healthy transcendent reason, he will evolve in the direction of celestial reason. Conversely, if he is controlled by the imperious impulses of the terrestrial soul, he will move in the direction of the terrestrial intellect and domination by the imperious self.

What, then, are the necessary conditions for the natural development and evolution of transcendent reason into celestial reason?

Above all, we must observe the health of the transcendent reason with the help of a correct education of thought, which results in basing our choices on correct principles—that is, ethical and divine principles that have reached us through the authentic teachings of the divine envoys. Authentic teachings educate us to distinguish between that which originates from the terrestrial part (the id) and that which originates from the celestial part (the ego, the superego, and the super id), making us aware of the principles we should apply, the limits we should observe, and the traps we should avoid.

By applying these principles, an individual gradually becomes aware of the rebellious impulses of his imperious self, for it is only through practice that our conscious will realize the existence of such impulses. The imperious self is an instinctual and thus tireless entity, whereas the celestial soul must exert willpower and effort to fight against it; consequently, if we remain negligent, the imperious self will automatically overtake and govern our entire being.

To succeed in this task, assistance from the Source is essential, for it is impossible without such help to repel the attacks of the imperious self (the impulses and illegitimate whims of the id). Divine assistance differs for each individual or group, but in general it is in the form of an energy that creates motivation within human beings to search for the truth.[2] This energy is essential for the regulation and acceleration of osmotic exchanges in the self. Without divine assistance:

♦ human beings quickly grow tired and lose their motivation;

♦ the osmotic exchanges of the self do not remain under the control of the celestial soul and fall into the hands of the imperious self;

♦ we lose, more importantly, the catalyst required for the transformation of our celestial character units into divine virtues.

In order to receive help from the Source, we have to tune our internal receiver to the divine wavelengths. To accomplish this task successfully requires "attention" to the Source, while it is our *intention* that determines how the energy that is received will be used.[3] Thus, to expend such energy in a positive way, we have to purify our intention, meaning we have to consider Him present in every situation and always seek His satisfaction.

Attention and intention thus play a vital role in the quality and application of the spiritual energy that is received. If an individual's attention is not directed toward the Source, he may receive energy that is of a different nature than divine energy, or even counter to it. On the other hand, if his attention is turned toward the Source but his intention is not divine satisfaction, the energy will be spent on futile ends.

In summary, the determining factors in the process of the transcendent reason's evolution into celestial reason are correct choices, perseverance, and divine assistance. If someone is un-aware of the authentic principles he must rely upon and does not know which path is correct, but has a pure intention nonetheless, the Source will arrange it such that his intention does not remain fruitless, and at the appropriate time and in the manner deemed best, he will be placed on the path toward his education. What is essential in this situation is one's intention, and a pure intention in any given task is seeking divine satisfaction.

ABODES OF THE SOUL

- ❖ Ascending Successive Lives

- ❖ The Interworld

- ❖ Coming Back on Earth

- ❖ Forgetting our Past Lives

- ❖ Death

- ❖ The Eternal Worlds

9. Ascending Successive Lives

The principle of successive lives is the key to the process of perfection.

The process of spiritual perfection in which the celestial soul develops until it completes its growth and reaches perfection is extremely long. During this process, the celestial soul is placed in the cycle of successive lives to acquire the requisite experiences for assimilating the various effects of the different levels of creation. For a number of reasons that will be discussed later, the initial stages of this process must be undertaken in a "material" environment, meaning that the human celestial soul must traverse the initial stages of its process of perfection here on earth. The celestial soul assumes an earthly body to lay the foundation of its educational stages for reaching spiritual perfection, even though in general it will attain perfection in another dimension—namely, the *interworld*.[1]

Laying this foundation is such an immense undertaking that it cannot usually be accomplished in a single earthly life, which is why human beings require numerous and successive lives to reach perfection. The succession of earthly lives is an ascending course in which human beings move in a progressive direction from one life to the next, provided that they use their free will correctly; we call this process *ascending successive lives*.[2]

General Principles

Ascending successive lives are governed by principles according to which everyone is allowed to benefit equally from the most suitable conditions for their process of perfection. Each person is allotted a set period of time on earth to complete the thousand educational classes (stages) in the process of perfection.[3] While it is not possible to exceed this allotted time, it is possible for someone to reach perfection, whether here on earth or in the interworld, before the end of this time limit. Reaching perfection on earth requires exceptional abilities and superhuman effort. Nevertheless, in rare, exceptional cases it is possible for someone to traverse the thousand educational levels in a single earthly life. In general, however, human beings need at least several lifetimes, if not the entire allotted time, to reach their goal.

In the interim between two earthly lives, we must necessarily spend a longer or shorter period of time in an intermediate spiritual world called the interworld, during which the positive and negative acquisitions from our different lives (on earth or in the interworld) are accumulated together. Thus, in addition to living in bodies A, B, C, D, etc., our acquisitions from those lives are also recorded in our being, without changing our identity or our feeling of self-awareness.

Each time we return to earth, a material environment called the **body-milieu** is designated for us based on what we have acquired in previous lives and what is suitable for advancing our spiritual education. The body-milieu is an ensemble composed of 1) the biological body, to which the terrestrial soul gives life, and 2) the environment, familial and sociocultural, in which we must develop. Therefore, to the extent of our free will, we contribute to determining the favorable or unfavorable conditions of our future body-milieu. By favorable conditions, we mean those that are favorable for one's spiritual development.

Special Cases

Ascending successive lives include special cases that are outside of the normal trajectory. For instance, it is possible for someone to merit not having to return to one or several earthly lives and, at the same time, to still enjoy their benefits.[4] Conversely, as a remedial measure it is sometimes necessary for malevolent individuals to be sentenced to one or several difficult lives marked by hardships, lack of faith, poverty, illness, debility, privation, frustration, etc.[5] Such penalties, which have a set duration and do not count toward the allotted time for the process of perfection, are designated for those who have knowingly, intentionally, and without regret committed inhuman acts such as repeatedly transgressing the rights of others, heinous crimes, etc. These individuals are placed in a situation where they can personally experience the same suffering they have inflicted on others so that their infirm souls may perhaps be cured and can once again travel the right path.

In general, although it is possible for the celestial soul to stop developing along the path or to even regress, ultimately it will never permanently descend to a stage below that of a human being. Since the celestial soul emanates from the divine breath, its creational rank is such that regardless of its errors, its nature will never change. For example, it will never transform into an animal or vegetal spirit, for its nature essentially differs from that of an animal or plant.

The following question may arise at this point: since human beings do not remember their past lives and are not aware of the cause of their penalties, what benefit could undergoing such penalties have? The answer lies in the fact that our positive and negative acquisitions from each life are recorded in their entirety in the unconscious; as the unconscious is constantly and actively interacting with the conscious, it becomes possible through this process not to repeat the actions and intentions that led to such reactions.

Successive Lives and Divine Justice

The fundamental pillar of creation is justice coupled with mercy, which is why beings innately yearn for justice. True peace is possible only when justice and equity prevail. If we do not believe in the principle of successive lives, many of life's events can engender a kind of rebellion or a sense of injustice within us. For instance, if we do not live more than once and if the Creator is just, how can we explain so many inequities? Why are some children born disabled, or why do they leave this world in their infancy with so much pain and suffering? Why, for example, do some people live in comfort and luxury? There are many such questions.

If we accept the principle of ascending successive lives, we will find convincing answers to such questions. For example, we will realize that the possibility of reaching the goal is the same for all individuals, that the current situation of each person is the result of his previous lives, and that the destiny of each individual depends on the merits he has attained through his own efforts. Understanding the existence of successive lives causes us to internally reconcile with the just and merciful Creator. With the knowledge that we gain, we will find convincing explanations for apparent injustices and will consequently be able to better endure them. If we have a better understanding of the cause of our sufferings and those of our fellow human beings, we can more effectively seek remedies and assist those who need help. At the same time, we develop confidence that our rights will never be trampled, which in itself will help us to become more serene, more optimistic, and more resistant in facing the ups and downs of life and not fearing death. Over time, we will develop certainty that whatever happens to us is just and in our own best interest. Ultimately, all of these truths go hand-in-hand until we become more diligent for the best thing possible: reaching perfection and joining the Source.

The End of the Allotted Time for Successive Lives

At the end of the allotted time for successive lives, several possibilities exist:

- ♦ Those who have reached perfection leave the causal universe[6] and return to their Source, where they will live in freedom and absolute eternal bliss.

- ♦ Those who have not reached spiritual perfection remain under the influence of causality and, depending on what they have acquired during the course of their lives, will join one of two worlds: if the balance of their actions is positive, they will occupy a level within the levels of paradise (the worlds of well-being); if the balance of their actions is negative, they will occupy a level within the levels of hell (the worlds of ill-being).

Regardless of the destination (paradise, hell, or perfection), no one will be subject to the final accounting without having had at least one opportunity in each earthly life to become familiar with authentic divine teachings. One of the main benefits of successive lives is that each individual is faced with divine truths at least once during the course of each lifetime—even if only for an instant—and benefiting from such opportunities depends upon the vigilance and choices of each individual.

The opportunities that are given to us to find divine truth constitute a level within the levels of the *divine argument*. These opportunities are repeated until an individual fully understands that he has certain duties here and has to fulfill those duties to reach spiritual perfection. Thus, we should be alert and not allow such opportunities to pass us by. While it is true that at least once in each lifetime there will be an opportunity to find the truth, recognizing such occasions requires attention. The truth may not be so evident, for example, and understanding it may require some scrutiny on our part, or it may be so fleeting that we have to immediately grasp it.

We have all heard many definitions of the Source. If His existence is not proven to us through what we have heard, it is our own responsibility to research and discover whether He really exists or not. Of course, it is possible to avoid this duty, but we should know that in the end our negligence will come back directly to us. It is impossible for the Source not to show His effects to anyone who invokes Him with sincerity, without prejudice, and without mental and intellectual rigidity. As soon as we take one step toward Him, He will open the door for us.

10. THE INTERWORLD

The other world is like a mirror; each person sees in it his own image.

B eings reside either in the material worlds or in one of the spiritual worlds.[1] The spiritual worlds—which are real, concrete, inhabited, structured, and hierarchical—are governed by an impeccable law and order coupled with divine mercy. These worlds are of such immensity and variety (in terms of populations and lifestyles, respectively) that they are beyond imagination, and great spiritual figures have discovered and discussed only small corners of them. In brief, the spiritual worlds are composed of 1) the interworld, where the souls of beings from every inhabited planet temporarily reside after they leave their biological bodies, and 2) the **eternal worlds** (the worlds of well-being, the worlds of ill-being, and the **Divine Entity**), which constitute the abode of souls whose allotted time for the process of perfection has expired.

The Interworld
Each inhabited planet has its own specific interworld located in the atmosphere of that same planet, only in a superior dimension. As such, the interworld is a continuation of life on that same planet, and everything exists in a more subtle but real manner.

Ostad Elahi describes the interworld of the planet earth as follows:

The interworld is located between the material world and the eternal worlds, which lie beyond the dimensions of time and space .... Even if all the beings of the universe, from the first to the very last, were gathered there it would not affect its relative space or capacity in the least …. In terms of the passage of time, a kind of time span exists for each individual according to his destiny and the merit of his actions. Depending on each individual case, it is possible for the duration of one year in the interworld to differ from that of one earthly year based on the solar calendar. For example, from one year to at least one second of earthly time could correspond to one second and at the most one year of interworld time, or vice versa. In addition, one should not imagine that time in the interworld—for instance, one second corresponding to one solar year in the material world or vice versa—is due to one's imagination or fantasy…. The axis of time and place in the interworld, which is a replicate world, is based on exhilarating and enduring spiritual effects, not material perceptions of volume and time belonging to the physical world.[2] Based on the foregoing, whatever happens for each person as a result of these spiritual effects is exactly like reality and the absolute truth.[3]

The Soul in the Interworld

The interworld is where souls reside after leaving their bodies. Our appearance in the interworld is the same as it was here, except that our body is replaced by a corporeal image, which is an exact replica of the biological body. Contrary to popular perception, the interworld, which is part of the "next world," is so real and concrete that it is terrestrial life that seems vague and dreamlike in comparison.

"The difference between the material world and the interworld … is comparable to the difference between a mother's womb for the fetus and the outside world for a newborn, or the difference between darkness and light."[4] Because we are free from the constraints of the physical body, our feelings and emotions are more profound and tangible, and we feel happiness and suffering far more acutely.[5] Nevertheless, despite having greater alertness and more profound and tangible feelings in the interworld, the mere fact of being liberated from the constraints of the physical body and entering the interworld does not increase our comprehension of the realities of that world. Over there, "each person sees his own image," meaning that souls in the interworld understand spiritual effects—whether pleasures or pains—the way they perceive them in their minds.[6] The interworld is located in a superior dimension, and to comprehend its realities it is necessary to cultivate the appropriate understanding of that dimension in this world. We enter the interworld with the same thoughts, the same education of thought, and the same **field of perception** that we have acquired here. In other words, we are the same there as we were here, and our degree of comprehension is directly proportional to the level of our spiritual education in this world (the quality of our education of thought). For example, when a true atheist enters the interworld, he is so preoccupied within the confines of his dark and narrow field of perception that he continues to deny, at least initially, the existence of the Source and other spiritual truths. The field of perception that he himself constructed and lived within in the material world has now turned him into an imprisoned being in his own mind and prevents him from establishing perceptual contact with his new environment.

After leaving the body and entering the interworld, several possibilities exist:

- ◆ An individual has reached spiritual perfection during the course of his life on earth—an exceptional but possible outcome—in which case he only passes by the interworld on his way to join the Divine Entity (the world of perfection).

- ◆ An individual has reached the end of the allotted time but has not reached perfection. In this case, he will be subject to a final judgment and will subsequently be sent to one of the worlds of permanent well-being (paradise) or ill-being (hell) based on what he has acquired during the course of his successive lives.

♦ An individual has not reached perfection and has not reached the end of the allotted time, in which case several possibilities exist, including:
—He may be kept in the interworld from a few seconds to several years or more before being returned to a new body-milieu.
—As a result of having acquired a sufficient level of spiritual education[7] in the material world, he may merit remaining in the interworld to continue his process of perfection there until he reaches perfection and joins the Divine Entity.

Residing in the Interworld

The duration and manner of an individual's residence in the interworld depend upon the quality of his education of thought[8] and his spiritual reserves.[9] The duration of his residence may last from a few seconds to several years, but regardless of how long it actually is, this period is not counted toward his allotted time on earth. How one resides in the interworld varies infinitely and differs according to each individual. To simplify, we will outline a few general cases below.

After death, someone who has acquired a certain level of merit will be sent to a provisional paradise.[10] Situated somewhere between the interworld and the eternal worlds, this paradise will appear to him in the same way that he had aspired to it during the course of his earthly lives, and is the same as that which his religion had taught him was the ultimate goal. After residing there for a period, the soul will discover that this paradise is not really the final goal, and will request to be sent back to earthly life so that it can increase the level of its education of thought in order to reach the ultimate goal.

For almost everyone, therefore, the interworld is an environment for education and assistance, with numerous opportunities for advancement. Over there, an individual can receive a spiritual education and increase his knowledge of divine truths, or he can continue his development by absorbing the effects that emanate from the material world (such as sensations, emotions, etc.). It is also possible for a soul in the interworld to be connected to a person on earth whose situation in terms of the environment, behavioral characteristics, etc., is similar to what the soul in the interworld would have had if it had been returned to earth. Through this connection, the soul in the interworld benefits from all the spiritual progress of the person on earth, without being accountable for that person's potential mistakes. In other cases, conditions similar to those of a terrestrial life can be arranged for a soul residing in the interworld, in which case the soul can continue its process of perfection by encountering its earthly sensations and emotions, but with the advantage of being more alert and more conscious of its situation and the necessity to progress; consequently, it will commit fewer mistakes and will work with greater motivation and enthusiasm.

Above all, then, the interworld is a world of lucidity, compassion, and mercy, even if there are those who must endure temporary penalties there for therapeutic reasons. For those who have deviated and become lost during their lives on earth, the interworld provides an opportunity to compensate, while for those who have made progress it provides tools for faster growth. Free from material constraints, we acquire an awareness of all that we are and all that we could be, and in an atmosphere filled with mercy, compassion, and mutual assistance, we are able to continue our progress.

11. Coming Back on Earth

The body is designated according to the soul's past account.

When a human being returns to earthly life to continue his process of perfection, he does not usually have a choice in the selection of his new body-milieu, which is designated according to various parameters, including one's merit and spiritual group.[1] Although an individual's request for a particular body-milieu may be considered if he has acquired sufficient spiritual reserves during his past lives, each person will be given what he deserves on account of his merit.

Factors that Influence the Psychospiritual Personality

The physical characteristics, essence, and psychospiritual personality of each individual is contingent upon seven factors, which are commonly known as the "creational factors":[2]

1. The individual hereditary (genetic) effect of each parent, grandparent, and great-grandparent (i.e., the fourteen ascendants) on the creational attributes of the child;[3]

2. The collective hereditary (genetic) effect of these fourteen ascendants on the nature and innate characteristics of the child, such that it becomes an independent and separate being from each of the constitutive elements of the parents and ancestors;

3. The effect of the parents' thoughts at the moment of conception;[4]

4. The effect of the nourishment of the parents at all times (prior to conception and during the mother's pregnancy);[5]

5. The effect of time and place at each moment;

6. The effect of family upbringing and the environment;

7. The effect of divine providence based on the child's inherent aptitude. (This is the determining factor, for it is divine providence that designates the appropriate celestial soul for each person. The more favorable the creational characteristics of the body, the stronger and better the celestial soul it will receive.)

Accordingly, every celestial soul that returns to earth assumes the body-milieu that it merits, meaning that at the moment of birth the body of a newborn receives the celestial soul it deserves. Considering that the celestial soul is the most important factor in the psychospiritual personality of human beings, we can appreciate the importance of these creational factors, as well as the major role parents play in the child's psychological and spiritual formation.

In general, if parents observe the creational factors that determine the characteristics of their children, they will receive a desirable (responsible, honest, wise, etc.) child that may even be luminous. The presence of luminous children benefits both their parents and society, and this positive effect will continue for the parents even after they have left this world. Such children possess a sound mind and are endowed with faith and integrity. Those who have served humanity and positively influenced society in some respect are among the group of luminous souls. Conversely, children with dark celestial souls can be a source of harm and discomfort for their parents, society, and even humanity at large.[6]

The Entering of the Celestial Soul into the Body

At the time of birth, usually when the newborn takes its first breath, the celestial soul enters the body and merges with the terrestrial soul, which has been present since the time of conception. For specific reasons, the celestial soul is sometimes forced to enter the body prior to birth, a situation that is extremely unpleasant for the soul. In some rare instances, the celestial soul may also enter the body at a later time, sometimes up to a few years after birth or, if the body lacks the necessary aptitude to attract the celestial soul, it may never enter it at all. An individual that is devoid of a celestial soul can be recognized by his lack of ordinary common sense and inability to discern between good and evil.

During the first few months of life, a newborn is unaware of its present state and continues to live in the consciousness of its former life, retaining some contact with the spiritual world. As it gradually becomes aware of its present state, the memories of its previous life begin to fade in its mind and it forgets who it was, gradually turning to its present condition. There are, however, certain children who continue to maintain contact with their **ultra-cerebral memory** (the memory of the celestial soul) and are able to retain specific memories from their past lives for a long period of time, sometimes even for their entire life.[7]

Regardless of the manner in which the celestial soul enters the body, it is an unpleasant experience, for the soul does not wish to leave the interworld and enter the material world. For the soul, coming to the material world is similar to being exiled from its abode—a familiar and extremely pleasant milieu—to a depressing, disagreeable, and harsh environment. Nonetheless, souls that are aware or sufficiently advanced are able to better accept returning to earth, for they know that this exile, however unpleasant, is temporary and beneficial. In fact, certain souls that have been given the option not to return to earth sometimes request to do so to be able to obtain certain spiritual benefits.

12. FORGETTING OUR PAST LIVES

The shock that the soul experiences upon enter-ing the body causes us to forget the memories of our past lives.

A Few Reasons Why We Forget our Past Lives
When human beings return to earth, they forget memories of their past lives for the reasons outlined below:

♦ If a child did not forget his past lives, he would necessarily continue to live in his past, and the process of adapting his self to his new body-milieu would therefore be severely impaired.

♦ One of the main reasons adults forget their past lives is the dark psychological veil that primarily results from the thoughts, feelings, and deeds that originate from the desires of their imperious self. When an individual is awake, this veil prevents communication between the conscious and the celestial soul.

♦ Another reason past lives are forgotten is divine providence, for if human beings retained memories of their past lives, it would disrupt the order and peace of the family unit and society as a whole. Suppose, for instance, that someone in his past life had transgressed the right of another individual and had oppressed that person, without the latter having been able to defend himself. Now, if the oppressed individual recognized his oppressor in his following life, he would be unable to prevent himself from seeking retaliation. It is to our advantage, then, to forget our past lives. In light of the fact that most individuals are unable to subjugate their impulses and emotions, if the memories of past lives were to remain in our minds, such chaos would ensue that life would become impossible.

♦ Still another reason is that if we did not forget our past lives, the memories of our different lives would be connected to one another and it would appear as if we had only one life. Now, if an individual were to go astray in one of his lives, for example, and be left behind spiritually, he would become discouraged and his despair would prevent him from compensating for this lapse. Such an individual would be like a marathon runner who has dropped so far behind his competitors and is in such despair that he wants to quit the race. Regardless of a person's spiritual situation, however, at least once in each lifetime he is given an opportunity to compensate for having spiritually fallen behind. It is even possible for someone to compensate for his entire past by performing just one positive act with good spiritual repercussions. Forgetting past lives enables us to benefit from the requisite hope and motivation to compensate for lost opportunities, and to take a step in the right direction each time with the necessary energy and enthusiasm.

The Ultra-Cerebral Memory

For the reasons outlined above, as long as human beings cannot control their nature (the impulses of the id) it is better for them not to recall memories of their past lives. All of these memories are nevertheless preserved in their entirety in our ultra-cerebral memory (the memory of the celestial soul), and we feel their effects in our present life through the unconscious, without necessarily being aware of this ultra-cerebral memory; this situation often explains certain fears, fantasies, intense attractions, extraordinary aptitudes, etc.

At the moment of death, everything an individual has experienced in this life or in past lives passes before him as though on a movie screen, and he experiences all of it again as if it were happening in the present. From the standpoint of earthly time, this recollection does not last more than a few moments, but from the viewpoint of the dying, the events take place in real time. Subsequently, the person enters the interworld and once again forgets his past lives, recalling only his last life.[1]

Even before leaving this world, those who have gained control over their instincts and emotions can establish communication with their ultra-cerebral memory and thus recall parts of their past lives. This is also true, however, of certain individuals who have not acquired such a level of self-control. For example, such instances have been found among children as a result of their greater purity, which is why some children have revealed specific details from their past lives that have later been verified. With the help of scientific regression techniques, it is possible to access certain passages from one's past lives and to even obtain information about the interworld. In such cases, the events that find their way to the conscious through the ultra-cerebral memory usually do not lead to undesirable consequences. Individuals rarely recall memories that are truly important or that may result in harm to themselves or disruption in the social equilibrium.

13. DEATH

There is no death. Like a seabird, we plunge beneath the water each time and resurface elsewhere.

The Sensation of Human Beings at the Moment of Death
The origin and natural abode of the celestial soul is the spiritual universe, and its coming on earth in the mold of a body is comparable to being exiled and imprisoned in a dark and narrow cell;[1] hence, death is generally accompanied by a feeling of liberation and relief. Nonetheless, the sensations felt by the dying when the soul separates from the body depend upon the quality of one's education of thought and the cause of death. Natural death (meaning a death that occurs at a designated moment pursuant to a normal destiny) is extremely pleasant and intoxicating, whereas sudden deaths such as those caused by suicide or certain tragic deaths are entirely disagreeable to the soul. In sudden deaths, the soul is not prepared to separate from the body and therefore does not understand what is happening: it usually remains in a state of confusion and bewilderment for a more or less lengthy period of time, without knowing who or where it is. To be liberated from such a state of ill-being quickly, there is no better guarantee than having faith in the Source.

If someone has received a correct spiritual education or has simply lived according to the voice of his conscience, his soul will leave the body easily and pleasantly at the moment of natural death. Liberated from the prison of its body, the soul feels light and elated, and though it may feel a little disoriented at first, this feeling will quickly dissipate upon being welcomed by its deceased relatives. In general, natural death is like a liberation for everyone,[2] while difficult and painful deaths occur for malevolent individuals who have made a habit of committing evil without any remorse.

Suicide

The biological body is like an innocent child whose guardianship has been entrusted to the celestial soul, meaning us, and we are therefore responsible for its life. In addition to constituting an act of disobedience, suicide is also considered an act of betrayal and a transgression: it is an act of disobedience toward a divine command, for He has prohibited human beings from committing suicide; it is a betrayal of divine trust, for He is the one who has entrusted us with this body; and it is a transgression of the rights of the body, for it is a precious, innocent, necessary, and beneficial creation. That is why all divine envoys have declared suicide as an unforgivable act. Understanding the reason for such rigidity may not be readily apparent, especially since most suicides are motivated by despair, pain, and suffering. However, finding oneself in such a situation is not coincidental either, and is often the consequence of certain grave acts committed in the past. Of course, some suicides, such as those committed by children or the insane, or those committed under duress, are looked upon with divine indulgence. Suicides committed out of despair or pessimism are among the most serious cases and entail indescribable suffering. The penalty for those who commit suicide depends upon their level of reason and comprehension, but it would be a mistake to imagine that there is any forgiveness in such cases.

At any rate, suicide is never a means for escaping any kind of suffering, whether physical or mental. No one is capable of ending his "self"—only the body can be set aside, never the "self." Whatever the reason for the suicide may be, when someone takes his own life, it is as if his soul has been suddenly and prematurely separated from its body. In such a state, the soul is like a wanderer left to itself at the border of the interworld, in a place resembling an infinite no man's land devoid of any horizon or life. Lost and disoriented, without any purpose or assistance, it has to remain in this state for quite some time, perhaps even years. In addition, throughout this time it continuously feels the suffering it had sought to escape, as well as the pain and physical suffering it endured during the actual suicide, such as the feeling of suffocation, etc. Only after completing these painful stages will the soul gain access to the interworld, where it will have to answer for its action.

Those who attempt suicide but do not succeed and are saved have definitely acquired some merit in the past, such as helping to save someone's life or other similar acts. As for those who promote the idea of suicide, they will share responsibility for the suicides they have encouraged and will suffer their consequences.

It has sometimes been observed that for no apparent reason the idea of suicide may even arise in certain individuals of sound mind. This may be due to the tremendous extent to which they are unconsciously eager to free themselves from the prison of the body. In such a state, they unconsciously desire to prematurely end their natural life. This thought may also be a reflection of the struggle between the celestial soul and the imperious self that is taking place in the realm of the unconscious. Unaware of spiritual realities, they are actually seeking to liberate the soul from the clutches of the imperious self by eliminating the body. When such individuals become aware of the existence of this inner struggle, their motivation to commit suicide usually disappears.

Once a person comes to the realization that his true self is not limited to his biological body and that he will continue his life after leaving this body, he should naturally start to think about acquiring things that he can use in his future life. To date, no one has been able to prove the nonexistence of the other world, whereas there have been numerous accounts that would prove the opposite. Even if an individual is still unaware of the existence of the other world, reason dictates that he adopt a prudent approach and at least consider its existence to be possible.

The spiritual worlds are precisely organized, governed according to their own specific laws, and in possession of their own particular values. The best things in the terrestrial world may not only be worthless in the spiritual world, but may even turn out to be a burden for us. Upon arriving in the other world, the first thing that is evaluated and more important than anything else is the quality of one's education of thought. For example, if a person has lived his life in this world without faith and without having made the effort to ascertain the correctness of his mindset, he will definitely be subject to humiliation in the other world. Of course, it is possible for someone to live in total ignorance and not have this issue even cross his mind, or to ultimately deny the existence of the Source as a result of encountering an erroneous and dogmatic religious education. In such cases, he will not be reprimanded for his lack of faith, but he will regret not having searched further to discover the truth.

It is therefore extremely important to understand that the death of the biological body is not the end of life, but rather the opposite—it is a rebirth. The more we have prepared ourselves to understand this reality, the more pleasant we will find it to be.

14. The Eternal Worlds

*The exhilarating effects of the world of perfection
are renewed each moment, none resembling the
other, each greater and more powerful than the last.*

The time allotted for the celestial soul to travel back and forth between the earth and the interworld in order to reach spiritual perfection is limited. Once this allotted time expires, human beings leave the terrestrial world permanently and without any regrets to join the other dimensions (worlds) and in reality undergo their own specific "Day of Judgment."[1] It is after this final evaluation (judgment) that each person joins his eternal abode. The meaning of the final judgment and the evaluation the divine envoys have spoken of thus becomes comprehensible in such a context.

Briefly, we can say that the eternal worlds (eternal spiritual universes) an individual enters after the final judgment consist of three main abodes: the world of perfection (the Divine Entity), the worlds of permanent well-being (paradise), and the worlds of permanent ill-being (hell). According to the stages it has traversed, each soul acquires its own place in one of these abodes—which have an infinite variety of forms and levels—that may be different from that of the others. In reality, the different levels of the eternal abodes correspond to the soul's proximity to or remoteness from the Source, which determines its degree of felicity or suffering.

At the ultimate level of spiritual progress (perfection), human beings join the Divine Entity, meaning the world of perfection. The faster a soul reaches perfection, the greater the distinctions it will enjoy.

If an individual does not reach perfection within the allotted time, he will undergo a final judgment at the conclusion of this period. All of his lives will then be weighed in the balance, and he must answer for the use he has made of his free will, transcendent reason, conscience, etc. The criteria upon which this judgment is based are not necessarily the moral and religious laws commonly accepted in this world, for many of these laws have either been set forth by men or have been subject to tampering over time and have been deviated from their true state; rather, the laws according to which one is evaluated are authentic divine laws that are all based on justice coupled with divine mercy.

The state of the soul during this judgment is indescribable, for at that moment it is completely conscious and sensitive, fully aware of the effects of this judgment on its eternal destiny. Considering that dignity and honor are among the primary attributes of the celestial soul, one can imagine how painful it is for the soul to tolerate blame, reproach, and regret. Inasmuch as the details of one's earthly lives are inscribed within the self, each person is fully aware of his state and his responsibilities. Hence, one wholeheartedly accepts the results of this judgment, even if it is unfavorable and bitter, without the slightest feeling of injustice. Souls then proceed to the level of eternal well-being or ill-being that they have come to deserve.[2] If, on the whole, their positive and negative points are equal, then out of divine clemency they will be placed in the lowest degree of the worlds of well-being.

The Worlds of Well-Being and Ill-Being

The sensations of well-being that exist in the different levels of paradise, and the pain and suffering that afflict the soul in the different degrees of ill-being, are truly ineffable. Divine envoys have only sketched a symbolic depiction of paradise and hell corresponding to the level of intellectual understanding of the people of their own time in order to encourage them to do good and to warn them against vile acts.

The worlds of well-being contain degrees and levels that surpass the descriptions presented in the holy scriptures. In reality, these texts merely provide a few hints to convey an image of this world, but whatever these eternal paradises may be, they are still far inferior to the world of perfection. Even at a high spiritual level, a soul's happiness and freedom is limited and relative in these paradises.[3] While it is true that an individual enjoys great happiness there, he will always long for the bliss of the world of perfection.[4]

The descriptions of hell one also finds in the holy scriptures are accurate, but they are limited to certain specific and pictorial aspects. In reality, hell is where one is discontent and suffering. Considering that the source of pain and suffering varies for different individuals, there is no single image of hell for everyone, and the degrees of suffering and torment vary. The suffering of hell can be of a physical or spiritual nature. One form of suffering there is an individual's own vision of his vile intentions and actions, to which is added the suffering that derives from the person's sense of blame and reproach.

So it is not the Creator that penalizes an individual, but the accumulation of his own willful, negative intentions and actions which, in accordance with divine justice, results in such a state. When the Source directly intervenes in the destiny of His creatures, it is always in the direction of mercy and indulgence. Thus, however eternal hell may be, and however innumerable an individual's misdeeds may be, divine mercy is always more eternal and more innumerable. That is why we can say the eternity of hell is relative, for divine forgiveness ultimately encompasses everyone. Nonetheless, the state of a pardoned soul is similar to that of an officer who, having been dishonorably discharged and sentenced to life imprisonment for the crime of treason, is ultimately pardoned; a trace of regret will always remain with him.

The World of Perfection

The world of perfection, or the Divine Entity, is the abode of those who join the unique Essence after reaching spiritual perfection.[5] There are so many degrees and levels in the world of perfection that it is beyond imagination; it is the highest and most sublime of all worlds. Its inhabitants have control over everything, and with total alertness and complete knowledge they enjoy infinite freedom and love in the vicinity of the Truth, as well as peace of mind and unlimited possibilities. Words cannot convey even the slightest state of joy and bliss that a perfect being feels in the world of perfection.

Whenever we speak of eternity, it is not meant in an absolute sense, for absolute eternity is specific to the unique Essence. The eternity of beings is relative, since anything that has a beginning must necessarily have an end.[6] Someone who reaches perfection, however, joins the unique Essence and, through permeation by divine eternity, becomes truly eternal.

FACE-TO-FACE WITH OUR DESTINY

- ❖ Evil

- ❖ Determinism and Free Will

- ❖ Variable and Invariable Destinies

- ❖ The Recording of our Actions and Thoughts

- ❖ The Consequences of our Actions

15. Evil

Consider every being as good, for none is bad in origin.

E vil is not a divine creation: it is a dysfunction resulting from the misuse of free will by responsible beings. The Creator could have avoided such dysfunction by making responsible beings subject to determinism and depriving them of any freedom or right of choice. Free will, however, is a grace bestowed upon human beings so that they may realize their spiritual growth through reasoning. Without free will during the process of development, there can be no reasoning, no mistakes, and no conscious experience, and without these elements there can be no transcendent perception or knowledge.[1]

Traveling the path of perfection and having to exercise free will necessitates the existence of opposites. It is by confronting opposites that one can become aware of the true meaning of each thing. For example, by confronting lying and cruelty one can come to understand the value of honesty and mercy. Thus, as long as there are beings endowed with free will, one should not expect the source of "evil" to run dry.

What is Evil?

In general, "evil" or "negative" refers to anything that harms the true rights of beings and causes a disruption in their process of spiritual perfection. The concept of evil is thus relative, and varies according to the creational nature of beings. In light of their spiritual dimension, evil for human beings refers to the ensemble of factors that deviates the direction of their spiritual movement toward the Source, or slows or stops such movement. Consequently, actions of the imperious self that are contrary to the development of the celestial soul are considered evil or negative for us. From the viewpoint of tenebrous beings, luminous souls—including the celestial souls of human beings—assume the role of negative forces. In reality, tenebrous beings can only harm humans when they are able to control them. Such beings are neither evil by creation nor inherently bad, and their existence is even necessary, for it is by struggling against their effects that we can advance in spirituality and reach our perfection.

The Issue of Satan

One of the Creator's attributes is being an educator, teaching and helping us to grow and develop. He educates beings through various means that are appropriate for their level of understanding and comprehension. One of His educational methods is the staging of "scenarios." When the Source wants to teach us a principle or lesson, He often creates a scenario, of which there are many examples in the holy scriptures. One such parable is the story of Satan (Azazel).[2]

After the Source created man from black mud, He insufflated him with a breath from His own soul, which bears the divine particle, and ordered all the angels, including Azazel, to prostrate themselves before man. All the angels obeyed but for Azazel, who did not see the divine particle due to his pride: "Man is created from clay and I from fire. How can fire, which is superior to clay, prostrate itself before clay?" The Source replied: "He who is closer to Me is superior." As a punishment for his disobedience, Azazel was banished and called Satan (rebel). Thereafter, his heart brimming with hatred toward human beings, Satan appealed to divine justice and sought his reward for his past acts of devotion: "I want dominion over human beings. I want to lead everyone astray and draw them toward hell. I want to be the ruler of the wealth and riches of this world. I want those like me to multiply and to match the number of human beings." The Source replied: "I will grant you this power, but you will never have dominion over those who bear the light of my faith in their hearts and who are sincere toward me; on the contrary, they are the ones who will have control and dominion over you and the likes of you, and I will forgive those who repent after succumbing to your temptations."

There are many precious educational points concealed in this scenario: the divine particle in the celestial soul of human beings represents the effect of the Source within them, while their diabolical effects stem from their imperious self, which instinctually imparts the proud and rebellious behavior of Azazel to them. The difference is that the imperious self bears no responsibility or accountability for its actions, as it has no substantive existence, whereas a human being (meaning his celestial soul) has to answer for the actions he commits under the influence of the imperious self.

Azazel also represents negative spirits and individuals, such as venomous human beings, as well as certain relatives and acquaintances who assume a negative role, including those who say things out of friendship and create doubt in one's faith.[3] All of these beings are like pawns of the negative force that penetrate human beings through the imperious self.[4] The most dangerous are the venomous individuals, who can be found at all levels of society, particularly in mystical and religious environments. They share the same characteristics as Azazel, and their appearance is so deceptive that they do not raise the slightest suspicion. They see the truth inversely (they consider truth as falsehood and falsehood as truth) and have an unconscious hatred toward saints and true believers. Their being and words emanate a negative and powerful anti-divine energy whose effect on the soul is like that of carbon monoxide[5] on the body, such that if someone were placed in a position to socialize with them or listen to what they were saying, he would become spiritually poisoned without realizing it himself. If this poisoning were to continue, it would cause the individual to gradually transform into a faithless person and even into a venomous human being (a source of spiritual poison).

In contrast to venomous human beings are individuals with luminous attributes. Their presence and words permeate one with affection toward the Source and positive energy, such that the effects of faith, serenity, benevolence, and an abundance of material and spiritual graces radiate in their surrounding environment. It is this positive energy that prevents the negative effects of human actions from ruining everything. The story of Lot is a testament to this, for as long as Lot was in the city of Sodom, it remained intact.

To avoid falling into the trap of venomous human beings, one must rely on the authentic teachings of true spiritual figures, have pure faith in the true Source,[6] and fight against the imperious self by receiving help from the divine energy and light. Under these circumstances, evil will not be capable of having a lasting influence on one's heart.

As for the evil committed by others, it is the conscientious duty of every individual to fight against it, just as it is every individual's duty as a human being to have empathy toward his fellow beings and not to spare any effort in helping them.

16. DETERMINISM AND FREE WILL

With the help of free will, we can overcome the determinism that governs our being.

In addressing the question of divine intervention in the destiny of human beings, there are two extreme positions and one intermediate position to briefly consider. On the one hand, it could be said that human beings have no influence on their destiny and have only an illusion of freedom: everything that happens to them—and thus all of their actions, words, and thoughts—stems from their destiny and everything has been determined ahead of time. On the other hand, one could say that by granting them reason and free will, the Source has set human beings free, and thus their destiny lies entirely in their own hands. By carefully observing the events around us, however, we realize that neither of these two extreme positions is applicable to the vast majority of human beings, and it is therefore more logical to choose an intermediate position, which is **the principle of the middle way**.[1]

The Principle of the Middle Way

If an individual reflects on the events in his own life, he will realize that some are the direct consequence of his own decisions and actions, while others have occurred for reasons beyond his control and even against his wishes. This opposition between human will and destiny can be explained by the principle of the middle way. According to this principle, to the extent that the Source has given us the faculty of discernment, the right of choice, willpower, and the freedom to act, each of us is responsible for his own destiny; at the same time, since a part of each individual's destiny depends upon divine providence,[2] some events lie beyond our will. For instance, someone builds a sturdy structure but an earthquake destroys it. Although such an incident is not merely coincidental, it is beyond one's control. On the other hand, if someone lives in a decrepit house with a cracked roof that eventually collapses because he neglected to repair it, there is no doubt that he himself is responsible for such an event. Or to take another example, if a good driver who observes all the traffic regulations nevertheless has an accident, it can be considered as part of his destiny, whereas for a careless driver such an explanation would not suffice.

While it is true the destinies of special groups such as children and the insane have generally been designated ahead of time, outside of these cases events in the lives of human beings are subject to the principle of the middle way, which governs both their material and spiritual lives.[3] With regard to their spiritual destiny, all the necessary tools for their spiritual advancement have been placed at their disposal so that they can reach perfection—the rest is up to each individual to make the correct decisions and to use these tools appropriately.

How We Approach our Destiny

The manner in which we approach our destiny is contingent upon the degree of our spiritual maturity. The more mature the soul, the more we are naturally submitted to the divine will, and the less we complain about our destiny. Gradually, we become aware that everything is subject to divine providence, which is based on justice and mercy.

Creation is governed by precise laws, some of which pertain specifically to the spiritual perfection of human beings. These laws are implemented through what is called *the divine system*, which is regulated in such way that no right is ever transgressed.[4] In this world or the other world, human beings always reap what they have sown. Divine providence thus takes shape through the functioning of the divine system, which generally responds on the basis of one's past and present intentions and actions.

Above all, divine providence is concerned with the improvement and protection of all creation, including human beings. An unpleasant incident, for example, can eliminate the undesirable effects of a wrong action from one's soul and destiny. Quite often, the Source erases our errors by causing us various hardships and troubles. These difficulties are warnings for us to avoid committing other mistakes and to preserve the health of our celestial soul. Thus, most of the seemingly unpleasant events are in reality kindnesses that are intended to purify and educate us spiritually. For example, when someone commits a grave error and immediately experiences its unpleasant reaction, he might become aware of the dangers of repeating that mistake and thus rectify himself. Some unpleasant situations are not related to our past, but instead are tests intended to either advance or protect us from a worse event or situation. Suppose a qualified person is not selected for an important position: with the passage of time, he comes to realize that this position could have placed him in a situation where he would have committed an irreparable mistake.[5]

Someone who truly understands divine providence and has heartfelt confidence in it realizes everything that happens to him is in his best interest and will help him in his spiritual progress. Such tests are in reality divine signs in order to facilitate his advancement. By adopting such a perspective, we become less bothered by the difficulties of life and more detached from material possessions. We experience less psychological pressure, become more optimistic, and confront life's problems more serenely and with a more profound view. Moreover, our reliance on the Source also increases, as His eternal, assuring, and loving presence becomes more tangible and we discover He is the best and most solid support for us.

Of course, such an understanding of divine providence should not draw us toward a distorted form of determinism and a passive state. For example, if someone falls sick and assumes it is the result of his destiny and does not seek to cure himself in the hopes of divine assistance, or makes an excuse that his sickness is the divine will and does not take any steps toward improving his health, he would be seriously mistaken, for the Source has provided us with the necessary tools to seek treatment. In any situation, therefore, the correct approach is as follows:

- To use all the legitimate tools at one's disposal in an intelligent way.

- In addition to being active, to be calm about the result and to know it is the Source that will determine the outcome based on one's merit. If an individual (by taking into account laws, norms, and ethics) does everything in his power and is still unable to fulfill his legitimate desire, he should not become upset, for he should know what the Source wants is best for him. In every situation, we should make an effort within the limit of our possibilities and the realm of legitimacy while, at the same time, realizing that outside the scope of our will lies another realm in which He acts in our interests.

In spirituality, there are three ways of approaching destiny and divine providence that are representative of the three main stages of a spiritual student's advancement.

The first stage is contentment in the general sense: through reason and with the help of self-suggestion and the power of faith, an individual tries to prefer divine satisfaction to his own satisfaction, for he is certain what the Source wants is to his advantage and thus tries to be mentally content with whatever the outcome may be. If the result of his efforts doesn't meet his expectations, he tries not to complain inwardly.

The second stage is surrender: the person wholeheartedly accepts the divine will. Such a state creates a serenity within him that becomes part of his nature. At the end of this stage, humility replaces pride, altruism replaces selfishness, detachment replaces attachment, forgoing pleasures replaces seeking pleasures and whims, etc.[6] He acquires control over the self and desires nothing but divine satisfaction. His will disappears before the divine will, and a state of serenity, satisfaction, and true submission manifests within him.

The third stage is contentment in the specific sense: at this stage the individual's will becomes the divine will (the stage of unicity), and he lives in a state of complete free will. In everything he does and thinks, the cause stems from the Source, who is with him at all times. It is only at this stage that he can feel a conscious and unconditional love for all creatures, for he sees the Source in everything.

Between the three stages noted above, there are deep ravines that make traveling from one stage to the next extremely difficult, if not impossible, for all but the exceptionally elite. Those who have come to know the **Divinity of the Time** can travel these stages easier, for they benefit from two other intermediate stages that have been placed between stages one and two and two and three.[7] In these two other intermediate stages, assistance from the Divinity of the Time facilitates passage from one stage to the next.

17. Invariable and Variable Destinies

Two factors determine our destiny:
intention-action and divine providence.

Destiny is a general current that encompasses all beings and moves them toward the Source (their origin). Responsible beings who possess free will fall outside of this current, however, for they can intervene in their destiny through their own choices.

The destiny of beings includes two facets: invariable destiny and variable destiny.[1]

Invariable Destiny

The events resulting from one's invariable destiny are immutable and will inevitably occur. The factors that determine one's invariable destiny are recorded on the protected or "invariable tablet," and the Source is the only one who knows of its contents and the only one who can change them. In some cases, He reveals parts of it to certain saints and others who are close to Him.

Any effort to prevent the events recorded on the protected tablet from transpiring or the divine will from being realized is futile. One of the signs of an invariable destiny is that its events lie outside the scope of the ordinary and seem unexpected. For example, many times we have seen individuals without the necessary merit enjoy exceptional success, while others encounter failure despite their greater merit.

The closer an individual is to the Source spiritually, the more the wavelength of his will is aligned with the divine will (his will becomes compatible with that of the Source), and the more the favorable destinies on his protected tablet increase. For this reason, the majority and sometimes even the entire destiny of certain divine envoys and saints is recorded on the protected tablet. For example, Moses' rescue by the Pharaoh's daughter, the moment of Buddha's "enlightenment," the birth and passing of Christ, or the important events in the life of Muhammad and the revelations that he received through Gabriel are among the well-known events that can be said to have been recorded on the protected tablet.[2]

Variable Destiny

Almost all the destiny of ordinary individuals is recorded on the "variable tablet." According to various factors—the most important of which are intentions, decisions (choices), and our daily positive and negative actions—the contents of this tablet are continuously in a state of flux and evolution. Human beings, then, are constantly changing their own destiny. For example, if an individual is destined to undergo some physical, spiritual, or material harm at a specific time, he can modify, change, or completely eliminate that harm through his actions. Consequently, each time an individual makes a choice between two options, he has directly intervened in his destiny, meaning that if his decision is geared toward a positive or ethical direction, the events on his variable tablet will be modified in his favor, or an unfavorable event on his variable tablet may even be nullified. Conversely, if his decision is geared toward satisfying the desires of his imperious self, his unethical or anti-divine behavior may negate a positive event that had been recorded for him on his variable tablet.

The combination of the seven creational factors through which each individual is formed is recorded on a person's variable tablet prior to conception.[3] Thereafter, up to the age of discernment, only the positive actions of a child are taken into account and have an impact on his future destiny. From that point forward, however, each person can change the course of his own destiny as a result of his free will. It is even possible for someone to modify or completely eliminate the effects of certain negative attributes—which have been engendered within him as a result of the creational factors and have an impact on determining his destiny—through positive actions that are geared toward that attribute. For example, after reaching the age of puberty, one can overcome a negative hereditary characteristic by applying the appropriate divine principle.

With regard to death, while it is generally not possible to delay the time of natural death, accelerating it lies within our control to a certain extent. If someone does not properly attend to his health (addiction to alcohol, tobacco, drugs, etc.) or is reckless in the face of certain dangers such as driving, he can accelerate the time of his own death. Each person is therefore responsible for his health and, to a degree, the duration of his own life.

Authentic saints can access some destinies on the variable tablet and even change them with permission from the Source. As for those individuals who possess some form of clairvoyance (like professional clairvoyants, mediums, etc.), they are able to see sparks of these destinies or sense the occurrence of certain events before they occur. Their predictions do not sometimes materialize, however, because although what they saw or felt corresponded with an instant from the instances of the variable tablet, they did not see the subsequent changes in one's destiny.[4]

It is also possible for someone to be informed through a dream about an unpleasant and at times difficult event forecast in his variable destiny. In such cases, it is possible to prevent the occurrence of that event or to diminish its impact by seeking help from the Source, especially through offerings, almsgiving, or other acts of devotion that correspond to an individual's beliefs and customs.[5]

Considering the destiny of individuals is usually recorded on the variable tablet, each person directly intervenes in his own destiny and can change a part of it at any moment through his actions and decisions. In practice, the more an individual attracts the divine regard, the more he sets a correct course for his destiny. Conversely, to the extent that an individual forgets the Source, the divine regard is equally distanced from him, and in such a state, without any guardian or protector, he is increasingly left to himself. Thus, the best way of positively intervening in one's destiny is to make an effort to recognize and act upon the rights and duties designated by Him and to seek divine satisfaction in every matter.

18. The Recording of our Actions and Thoughts

All our thoughts, words, and actions are recorded forever.

Nothing perishes. Every instant of our lives is forever recorded in the material world, the spiritual world, and especially in our own being, in a live manner as though it were being filmed.

Every action and word remains in the material world in the same way that a sound or image is recorded on a magnetic tape. The day when science is able to retrieve these recorded events from space and matter, we will be able to discover exactly what was said and done in the past. In addition, the earth, the atmosphere, objects, etc., record within themselves both the pleasant and unpleasant effects of the events they have witnessed. For example, sites where negative or tragic events have occurred radiate a negative energy that receptive individuals can sense, whereas sites that have witnessed positive and beneficial events radiate a positive energy that engenders a sense of comfort and joy in those who encounter it. If a site has been tainted with a negative charge, it is possible to neutralize that effect through the help of certain positive acts.[1] Authentic divine saints can also convert tainted sites bearing a negative charge into a favorable environment through their presence. Concealed within some of these saints is a positive force so powerful that with a mere glance or word, or simply by passing through a location (if they will it), they can permeate it with positive energy. This same force can also transfer positive energy to an object or food.[2] After leaving this world, the site or region where the bodies of such saints are memorialized is always imbued with a positive and beneficial energy.

The spiritual world is another recording device, but one far more precise than the material world. In addition to our actions and words, our thoughts, intentions, and feelings are also recorded in this dimension. In other words, all our thoughts, words, and actions throughout the course of our lives are recorded and archived in the spiritual world in a live and tangible manner, such that when we refer to them we will find them so real we will feel as if we have once again returned to those scenes and are reliving them.

Even more important than the two recording devices stated above is our own "being" or psychospiritual organism, which completely preserves within itself everything we have experienced, and are currently experiencing, in our lives. Another recording device that should not be disregarded is the material body. Each cell, organ, and member of the human body is endowed with a memory that bears witness to everything that has happened to it during the course of its life.

It is because of these various recording devices that at the moment of death, the events that have transpired in this life and in previous lives appear before us in full detail and in a live manner, as though on a movie screen or a theater stage.

In summary, everything we are and everything we have done is recorded and archived in our being, creating what we could call our "bar code." As soon as we enter the other world, the "designated agents" immediately become aware of the details of our lives by reading this bar code and are thus able to precisely determine our level and worth.[3]

In the other world, if someone does not merit having certain shameful acts concealed by the Source, they will remain unveiled and others (authorized souls) will be able to see them. Consequently, a bitter feeling of abjection will overcome us, for a sense of dignity and honor are among the predominant attributes of the celestial soul. We should therefore remember that each time we knowingly and intentionally transgress someone's right—whether through our thoughts (negative thoughts), our words (speaking ill of others, accusations), or our actions (various betrayals)—the time will come when we will be confronted with that individual, and he will clearly see what we have done to him. One can imagine the painful sense of shame that we would feel in such a state. On the other hand, if we compel ourselves to observe divine ethics and set divine satisfaction as our goal, we will be welcomed with respect in the other world and the points that we have acquired will transform into a source of love, honor, and bliss for us.

19. THE CONSEQUENCES OF OUR ACTIONS

If our intention is to attract divine satisfaction, it will prevent the reaction to our mistakes from ultimately being to our detriment.

To progress on the path of spiritual perfection in the best way possible, we must become familiar with the consequences of our actions. Once we realize the importance of the implications of our actions and become certain that the reaction to every action will come back to ourselves, we will be encouraged to do good and avoid malevolence, and will thus resist the desire to perform negative actions. Moreover, if we are mindful, we can always ascertain the rightness or wrongness of our course based on the signs that are usually present in the repercussions of our actions. Thus, every occurrence in life takes on a specific meaning and guides us toward the discovery of a higher dimension, such that we feel the reality of that dimension's presence at every moment.

Every action and thought, whether positive or negative, has at least one reaction and can entail additional consequences as well, including the result of an action, the repercussion of an action, the chain effect, and the substantive effect.

The Reaction to an Action

Every action has a reaction, whether immediate or delayed, regardless of the motivation and circumstances behind the action. A reaction may manifest through physical means (for example, we gossip about someone and "happen" to bite our tongue!) or through a psychological effect (as a result of performing an altruistic act, for example, we feel joy for no particular reason). Usually, there is a correlation between the type of action and its reaction. Although this connection may sometimes be quite clear (someone breaks a window with his fist and injures his hand, for instance), often we are unaware of the reactions to our actions.

The Result of an Action

The result of an action is determined by its spiritual value and more or less corresponds to the concept of "reward" and "punishment." The spiritual value of an action is contingent upon numerous criteria, including intention, the quality of an action, and particularly evaluation by the Source, which is the most important element and based upon divine justice and mercy. The result of an action can also be immediate or delayed; in the latter case, it will be acquired at a later time in this world or the next. Moreover, the result of an action can also be material or spiritual in nature: material results are acquired in this world, whereas it is possible to obtain spiritual results in both worlds.[1] An example of a positive spiritual result in this world is being guided toward the truth and safeguarded from choosing a strayed spiritual path.

In evaluating the result of an action, intention takes priority over the action itself. For example, if someone performs a good deed by helping another person solely with the intention of being ostentatious or receiving praise and admiration, the result he derives from his good deed will be the social respect he had sought, whereas if he had performed that same action without any expectation and solely out of altruism or for the sake of divine satisfaction, in addition to a material result (social respect) he would also have earned a spiritual result that would have counted tenfold at a minimum.

Often, it is the combination of several results that determines the tangible net result of an action. Accordingly, a small discomfort or hardship might be the result of a grave negative action that has been diminished due to a positive action (a munificent act, for example). In addition, by virtue of divine mercy, the result of positive actions is usually counted severalfold, while the result of negative actions is counted only once.

The Repercussion of an Action

The repercussion of an action constitutes the effect our actions have on others. Such an effect, which impacts the individual himself, is unavoidable.

For example, someone who lies loses the confidence of those around him, or someone who creates a useful invention will receive positive energy each time others benefit from his invention.

If an action is endowed with a divine effect, its repercussions will become more radiant as time passes. To better understand this concept and how the spiritual repercussions of some actions have impacted the world, it is helpful to look back on history. Upon a divine command, for instance, Abraham built a simple structure (the house of Kaaba) in a barren desert: years later that same structure would become the site of worship for Muslims world-wide. Jesus Christ, who had only a handful of followers during his lifetime and whose mission lasted but a few years, succeeded in laying the foundations of a great spiritual civilization without any material power. Today, not only is he revered by all Christians, but he is also respected by the followers of other religions. Thus, from apparently insignificant spiritual events, vast repercussions can unfold. That is why certain individuals with seemingly no material opportunities or means determine the course of humanity's destiny, whereas many of the most powerful people of this world perish without any lasting trace.

The Chain Effect

There are certain actions that may produce a chain (successive) effect. Based on the principle of sequentiality and succession, every action creates the possibility of performing a similar ac-tion. Accordingly, a positive action engenders the possibility of another positive action, whereas a negative action often places an individual on a course toward performing another negative action, a process that can continue until either a positive compensatory act or divine intervention breaks this negative sequentiality and succession.[2]

The Substantive Effect

The effect engendered in the psychospiritual substance of an individual as a result of repeating positive or negative actions is called the substantive effect. Repeating negative actions ultimately leads to the poisoning of our psychospiritual substance, while the repetition of positive actions facilitates our spiritual growth and strengthens the desire to perform more positive actions.

The combination of the substantive and chain effects gradually increases the intensity of the effects of our actions, whether in a positive or negative direction. Many felons, for instance, began their careers by committing petty crimes before becoming notorious criminals. Similarly, we must repeatedly fight against the minor desires of the imperious self in order to ultimately acquire the power to control its major desires.

Thus, every action can bear positive or negative consequences. We sometimes see individuals, however, who harm others and repeatedly engage in misconduct without apparently experiencing the consequences of their actions. In reality, although the Source completely encompasses all of His beings and is omniscient, He can nevertheless choose to disregard certain individuals. If, despite repeated warnings, such individuals persist in their misconduct and harming of others, they will be left to themselves in this lifetime—one of the worst spiritual penalties—and consequently will continue their vile acts without worry or fear. These individuals increase their burden daily and their psychospiritual substance (the soul) gradually becomes darkened and damaged, such that only the Source knows how and when they will have to compensate for all they have done.

It is extremely important to pay attention to the various implications of our actions, although in the beginning it is impossible to analyze each of the effects of our actions. In general, each act is considered a specific case, and countless material (circumstances, environment, personality, etc.) or spiritual (the true value of an action, intention, etc.) factors play a role. If the consequences of our actions are broken down and analyzed in this chapter, it is to provide a general overview of the subject. The reality, however, is that such implications are often mixed together and are simultaneously influenced by external effects. Only He who sees and is aware of everything can gauge the true value of each action and harmonize its implications.

Consequently, the wisest approach is to have a benevolent intention in every action and to strive to act in accordance with our conscience and divine satisfaction.

LIFE IN SOCIETY

- ❖ Our Conduct in this World

- ❖ Realism and Positive-Seeing

- ❖ Men and Women

- ❖ The Education and Upbringing of Children

20. OUR CONDUCT IN THIS WORLD

> *The cornerstone of life in this world is respecting the rights of others.*
> *No right is ever lost, for the Source is its Guarantor.*

The material world is a school for gradually undergoing the stages in the process of spiritual perfection. The "educational classes" consist of our family, friends, society, workplace, nature, etc. Our own being constitutes the "laboratory" for such classes, while our experiences and "examinations" are the tests we confront in daily life. To benefit from the best "education" possible, it is necessary to have access to divine guidance.[1]

During this educational process, experience plays a prominent role, for spiritual maturity, like intellectual maturity, is not acquired merely with theoretical knowledge. For example, one cannot come to know the Source simply by reciting prayers and praising Him; rather, one must *act* upon divine ethics and prescriptions—which constitute the food of the celestial soul—in the midst of society and in contact with others for the celestial soul to develop, mature, and thus come to know the Source. Similarly, one does not become tolerant or courageous by reading a few things about tolerance or courage: it is by acting upon these virtues within society for a sufficient period of time that we can assimilate them within ourselves. Spiritual education is similar to university studies in that each time we succeed in making a divine virtue appear within us, we have completed the spiritual credit for that virtue.

Material Life and Spiritual Life

Material life and spiritual life are often considered as separate or even opposing categories, though this is not at all the case. Natural spirituality—one based on the nature of human beings—is carried out in the current of daily life and is mixed with all the activities of material life, from insignificant details to vital decisions. **Divine spirituality** is an internal matter, not a superficial undertaking, and involves heartfelt intentions and the "whys" that lead to making decisions and performing actions. For example, the act of providing our child with an excellent education and upbringing may stem from the desire to satisfy our own pride and the intention to boast to others. Yet, this same action could be based on a spiritual intention and the desire to truly perform our spiritual duty so as to raise an individual who will be beneficial for society. These two apparently identical actions have neither the same spiritual value nor will they produce the same effects. Or to take another example, someone may desire wealth solely to satisfy his personal whims, whereas another person may have the additional intention of helping the needy as well.

Thus, from the moment our decisions, behaviors, and actions transcend the realm of purely animalistic impulses and our conscious willpower becomes inclined to act humanely, our life takes on a spiritual aspect. That is when materialism assumes its proper place—as a tool for progressing in spirituality and not as a goal in itself—and we become aware of our true level and fundamental goal.

Material life is like a spiritual goldmine for someone who knows how to benefit from it, which is why withdrawing from the world and living in seclusion is not an appropriate path for gaining proximity to the Source. In this day and age, having an active and beneficial material and social life, coupled with a spiritual intention, is more efficient, productive, and acceptable than secluding oneself and spending one's time solely on prayer and spiritual visions.

Principles and Duties

For our social and material lives to be spiritually beneficial, we must adhere to certain principles and perform certain duties, the most important of which are the following:

Principles

- Respecting the prevailing social laws and adhering to the norms of the society in which we live to the extent that they do not harm our spirituality; in other words, adopting a normal life and an appropriate behavior.

- Being mindful of the material and spiritual consequences of every action before performing it, and exercising caution and sound judgment in all matters.

- Seeking to establish equilibrium in our affairs. The soul and the body each have rights, which we have a duty to observe. Based on the principle of equilibrium, repressing the body for the sake of the soul is just as harmful as ignoring the soul to pursue physical pleasures. Someone who takes the principle of equilibrium into account will not abandon his family and social life for what he deems to be spirituality, and will likewise be careful that the attractions of material life do not preoccupy and distance him from spirituality.

Duties

The duties of human beings can be categorized as follows:

- Duties toward oneself (both one's celestial soul and terrestrial soul). An example of a duty toward the terrestrial soul is being mindful of one's physical and psychological health.

- Duties toward the Creator, which involve the relationship between human beings and the Source (to consider Him present and observant at all times and to observe the principles that have originated from Him).

- Duties toward others, which are prioritized as follows: our duty toward our spouse, children, parents, relatives, friends, society, etc. At the same time, as human beings we should not forget our duties toward other beings, including animals, plants, objects, etc., for each of them also has rights.

Observing the rights of others is the main pillar of family and social life and is applicable in all aspects of human relationships—it even includes social etiquette in daily life, which is why apparently small gestures like saying hello to someone or responding to a greeting carry their own particular importance. Overall, observing the rights of others requires the application of several ethical principles, including keeping one's promises, repaying ethical and material debts, and avoiding gossip, hostility, plotting (conspiracy), accusations, false rumors, etc. Among the ethical obligations that have been emphasized are gratefulness toward our parents and those who have taught us something or educated us in a benevolent manner, as well as all those who have sincerely helped us.

It is a divine law that no right will ever perish, for the Source serves as its guarantor. Human beings, therefore, have to be especially mindful not to infringe upon others' rights, for by knowingly transgressing someone's right we encumber an indebtedness to that person which we will have to repay sooner or later—whether in this life, subsequent lives, or in the other world. In such cases, we cannot merely resort to divine mercy, for the Source only forgives the debts we have incurred as a result of shortcomings in our duties toward Him. Every being whose right has been infringed, however, retains the inherent right to choose to forgive the transgression. For instance, if we intentionally and unjustly wrong someone, we will become indebted to that person, and as long as he does not forgive us, our debt will remain. Conversely, if someone is unjustly wronged, the oppressor will become indebted to him and no one but the oppressed can forgive him. That is why no right ever perishes in the divine system. Of course, the more advanced a soul becomes, the more it derives pleasure from forgiveness rather than revenge. At any rate, each person is free to choose whether or not to forgive an infringement of his right. The Source forgives, and He rewards those who forgive as well.[2]

In Search of Equilibrium

One of the spiritual benefits of living in the material world is the constant necessity to discern and observe our various duties and rights. For example, when we are in a dispute with someone, we have to know how and to what extent to defend our rights, without being excessive and infringing upon the other person's rights. Similarly, we have to know under what conditions we may forgo our own rights, without it being an act of weakness, cowardice, naiveté, or foolishness. We have to be vigilant in every situation, and find the proper balance in each case with the help of our reason. If someone wants to forgo his right, for instance, he has to be mindful that such forbearance does not irreparably harm him; that it is limited only to his own rights and does not harm a third person or society; and that the other person merits an act of forbearance.

Weighing our rights and duties is immensely educational, for in order to conduct ourselves prudently and wisely we must necessarily fall over and over again! Establishing equilibrium between our rights and duties is an art that is realized gradually through education, reflection, action, and repetition. It is clear that if we do not have access to correct basic principles as a reference, or make no diligent effort to apply such principles, it is doubtful that we can make any notable progress and reach the goal.

A Golden Rule

Performing duties and observing rights may seem impossible at first, for we do not have a set of instructions we can refer to in various situations. Nevertheless, among the pillars of theoretical and practical ethics is a golden rule that will make things easier if taken into account: *in every situation, put yourself in the place of others.*

In practice, this rule means that we should compel ourselves to wish well for others as much as we do so for ourselves. In other words, to wish for others every good we wish for ourselves, and to refrain from wishing any misfortune for others that we do not wish for ourselves, while being as diligent in defending the legitimate rights of others as we are in defending our own. The simplicity of this rule should not cause us to err and create the perception that we can apply it in any manner we like without using our faculty of discernment. The goal is not to satisfy whatever others may desire, but rather to avoid treating others the way we do not want to be treated ourselves. Being considerate of our neighbors and refraining from making excessive noise, for instance, is a simple and primary duty that we expect others to also observe in relation to us. If we do not want anyone to gossip about us, we should avoid gossiping about others; if we do not want anyone to make accusations against us or to ridicule us, we should not accuse or ridicule others; if we do not want anyone to divulge our secrets, we should not divulge the secrets of others; if we do not want anyone to conspire against us, we should not conspire against others; if we want someone to help us when we are in difficult situations, we should not refrain from legitimately helping others; and so forth.

By observing this golden rule, we not only help others, but in reality ourselves, for our conscience is at peace and our heart at ease. Internally, we always feel cheerful, lighthearted, and serene, and our problems are resolved easier. We enjoy a more successful family and social life, and become less unstable in our daily tasks. By cultivating kindness, benevolence, well-wishing, and other such attributes within ourselves, we attract divine grace and repel negative energies from our lives.

Hidden in the heart of every human being is a divine particle; consequently, attracting the hearts of others is attracting divine grace.

21. Realism and Positive-Seeing

A pessimist is deprived of seeing the truth.

*R*ealism refers to seeing things as they really are and observing events the way they have actually happened,
without falling into the abyss of naive optimism or misplaced
pessimism. The complement to realism is *positive-seeing*,
which means paying attention to and seeing the positive aspect
of each thing or event; this sense is one of the factors that prevent
bitterness in life.

Realism

To acquire the ability to see things realistically, each person must
first come to know himself better. To do so, we must focus within
and carefully evaluate ourselves until we better understand our ethical characteristics—that is, the strong and weak points of our
psychospiritual personality. It is these "characteristics" that constitute our self and our outlook. For example, if we find signs of
pessimism, we should make an effort to eliminate them. A pessimist
does not see positive aspects, which in turn causes him not to look
at things realistically and to be deceived by his incorrect judgments.
Naive optimism is the flip side of the same coin: a naive optimist
lives in the clouds and often overlooks realities. Aside from the foregoing, other factors that prevent us from seeing things realistically
include our dogmatic biases and preconceptions, whether scientific, religious, or otherwise, for they unduly influence our judgment
and perspective.

Positive-Seeing

Positive-seeing means to always perceive the good aspect or positive point in every event or thing, even in those that may seem unpleasant or negative to us.

"The Source has not created evil; evil is a consequence."[1] Since no being is created bad, there are certainly many positive qualities in all persons and things. To develop the sense of positive-seeing, we must continue searching for such positive qualities until it becomes our second nature. If we pay close attention, we can still find such attributes even in the presumably worst beings who, if aided in developing the positive aspects of their self, may turn into benevolent individuals in the future.

Likewise, we can find a positive aspect in every event, even the most unpleasant, which is why failures and deprivation can result in strengthening our personality and increasing our empathy toward the pain and deprivation of others. Or, it is possible for a minor hardship to preserve us from a grave accident. Imagine, for instance, two drivers traveling at the same speed when one of them is pulled over and issued a speeding ticket. After the driver resumes his course, a few miles down the road he comes across an accident involving several cars, one of which is the same car that had been next to him before he had been pulled over.... The distress caused by the issuance of the speeding ticket was in reality a blessing to preserve him from this impending danger.

To develop positive-seeing, we have to make an effort to refine our psychological personality. For example, we have to refrain from gossiping, whether actively or passively, and if the opportunity arises, we should even seek to defend those who are the subject of gossip. To do so, however, we must necessarily find some positive points in those we are defending, an act which in itself will slowly help us become accustomed to seeing the good. Another exercise for developing positive-seeing is to fight against our jealousy.[2] The appropriate way to fight against jealousy—which leads us toward malevolence—is to stand before an imaginary mirror and to see our own reality in it, meaning to try and evaluate ourselves sincerely and to carefully find all of our strengths and faults. In doing so, each person will find characteristics and advantages that he does not see in others and, consequently, if he is fair his jealousy will subside. In addition, if we have a correct understanding of spirituality, we can remind ourselves that no one is given anything without first meriting it, and if someone enjoys certain benefits he has definitely acquired the worthiness for them, whether in this life or in previous lives. Furthermore, we, too, can acquire such merit. On the other hand, being deprived of a benefit may not be related to a lack of merit, but rather that it is in our best interest not to have that benefit.

By developing the sense of realism and positive-seeing, our perspective toward the world changes, and we better understand the presence of a powerful and equitable Source and the role of His providence in our lives. As a result, we will become less jealous and more forbearing, and will complain less about our destiny, others, and the world in which we live. In such a state, we will become happier in life.

22. Men and Women

Once a marital union is established, a man and woman develop a physical and spiritual responsibility toward each other.

Men and women are created equal. "Equal" does not mean "identical," for each is endowed with his or her own specific characteristics and qualities. Affection, tenderheartedness, and spiritual sensitivity, for example, are more prominent in women, while men are usually more stable and less impressionable. Each of them also has specific weak points: vengefulness for women, lasciviousness for men. In the spiritual domain, however, men and women have the same possibilities of reaching perfection, at which point such differences no longer exist.

Marital Life

The union of a man and woman lays the foundation of their material and spiritual life, although this is not a general rule. There are many individuals, for instance, who do not get married and yet are extremely successful in their material and spiritual lives. Imposing celibacy upon oneself is not advisable unless one is naturally devoid of sexual desire or social factors prevent the person from getting married—for example, not having the opportunity to marry the person of one's choice, or finding a mutual life difficult to tolerate.[1] Men and women complement one another, and their union, if appropriate, will have an extremely positive effect on their social and spiritual lives.[2] Making a joint life official through the act of marriage is intended to highlight the commitment to perform the responsibilities of a mutual life.

When choosing a spouse, common sense, reason, and logic increase the likelihood of a successful marital life. If a couple's motivation is solely physical attraction and they marry on a whim, their differences will soon become manifest as their carnal passion subsides. On the other hand, a union entered into with the intention of forming a mutual, responsible life will have a greater likelihood of success. Choosing a spouse should not be based solely on material criteria (physical appearance, social status, etc.) but mainly on rational criteria, such as psychological, intellectual, and social affinity.

If the members of a family are united and sincere, they will attract the "divine regard," which will protect them. This regard often manifests in the form of a beneficial (positive) energy, in some traditions called the "angel of the home." On the other hand, a house filled with discord and hypocrisy (arguments, lies, deceit, etc.) attracts beings with a malevolent (negative) energy that create problems in the material and spiritual lives of the family members, causing family disputes, illnesses, unpleasant events, loss, lack of bounty, and so forth.

To succeed in marital life, a husband and wife should not lie to one another, should not unnecessarily involve others in their personal marital difficulties, and should not allow a third person to interfere in their private affairs. If a married couple becomes accustomed to solving their own problems, their difficulties will usually work themselves out, unless they are not appropriate for one another from the outset. Nevertheless, if things get to the point where a consultant is needed, they should seek someone who is neutral, experienced, and familiar with family psychology.

In addition to the foregoing, success in marital life requires observance of the following points as well:

♦ Each spouse should respect the rights and personality of the other.

♦ Each spouse should consider that half of him or her belongs to the other. Neither should hesitate in showing forbearance toward the other, and each should try to act in a manner that pleases the other.

♦ If a dispute arises, each of them should take the initiative in resolving it and neither one should display inappropriate pride.

♦ It is better to make important decisions together, taking into account the expediency of each spouse.

♦ The work and pressures of family life should be equitably divided between them.

♦ A husband and wife should be familiar with the psychology of the opposite sex, and at all levels of their life together each should keep in mind the other's nature and temperament. This is one of the fundamental factors in having a mutual understanding between them.

♦ They should exchange their views with one another and interact in such way that doing so becomes second nature to them.

If, despite all of the above, a dispute between a married couple remains and a mutual life becomes intolerable, it is better for them to separate and in doing so to observe each other's rights.[3] It is preferable not to rush or force the separation, but rather to take into account the condition and situation of the other person and to separate from one another willingly and on good terms.

Beyond physical attraction, when a true feeling of friendship and trust is established between a couple, we can say that the union is a successful one. The psyches of men and women complement one another, and the union of the two creates a tremendous force. When a husband and wife are united, therefore, their union becomes a support for their social life and endows them with self-confidence and power. Even in the spiritual domain, it facilitates their progress in the sense that their advancement becomes more balanced, more rapid, and less dangerous.

Children

Carnal desire aids in the unity of two complementary beings (man and women) and leads to reproduction, while the affection of parents for their children results in preservation of the species. As long as both parties are in agreement, there is no prohibition against birth control.

The psychospiritual capabilities of a child often depend on the nature of the relationship between the parents. A child who is born into a suitable environment that stems from the unity of the parents differs from one who is conceived as a result of a passing relationship or by force.[4]

The thoughts of the parents at the moment of conception also have an effect on the gametes: the energy of thought at that instant transfers its effects to the gametes (similar to the effect of light on photographic film). As such, it is better to have positive thoughts at the moment of conception; at the same time, being joyous during that period will also have positive effects on the psyche of the child.

The family environment has a tremendous impact in shaping the psychospiritual personality of the child, as well as his material and spiritual future. Spiritual education enters the soul through the psyche, and the foundation of each person's psychological personality is formed during childhood within the family environment. It is for this reason that the education of children plays such a fundamental role.

Parents have three major responsibilities toward their children:

1. Providing a correct ethical education and cultivating a true faith within them.

2. Providing for their material needs until they reach the legal age, and thereafter for as long as they continue their education.

3. Providing the grounds for an education or the learning of a vocation or trade.

If parents neglect these responsibilities, they will incur an unpardonable debt. For example, if a child denies the existence of the Source due to the parents' negligence or turns to wrongdoing, the parents will also share in the responsibility for those errors.

When a child reaches the age of responsibility and is able to provide for his own livelihood, the duties of the parents come to an end, and it is better for them to separate their lives at that point.

Children also have duties toward their parents: obedience, respect, and caring for them in times of need, especially during their elderly years. It is a child's responsibility to pray for the souls of his parents, whether during their lives or after their passing. Children are greatly indebted to their parents, whose blessing or curse therefore has a definitive impact on their lives.

An individual's duties toward his family follow a certain hierarchy: each person must first consider the prosperity and comfort of his spouse, followed by his children and then his parents.

Accepting the responsibility of family life carries a great spiritual benefit. By way of comparison, the spiritual value of one day in the life of someone who has accepted the burden of family life is equivalent to a thousand days in the life of someone who has withdrawn from the world and spends all his time in celibacy and seclusion.

Marital life is one of the pillars of society. This union creates the seed for material and spiritual life: if the seed is bitter, the fruits of the tree will likewise be bitter and damaged, but if the union is based on ethics and divine principles respected by both parties, the tree will produce fruits that are sweet and beneficial in every respect.

23. The Education and Upbringing of Children

One who can raise a child well can govern a country.

Experience has shown that the effects of a person's education and upbringing during early childhood bear a lifelong impression on his personality.[1] In addition to the ethical education and training of children, parents must also provide them with a spiritual education, for "ethics without the Source is like a tree with few roots" that will fall with the first strong gust of wind.

In the ethical education of children, instilling a sense of character and self-respect is the most important factor, as well as teaching them dutifulness, respect for the rights of others, fidelity to one's promises, honesty (without being naive), a sense of responsibility, etc.

In the spiritual education of children, we must gradually familiarize them with a few principles about the Creator, the other world, knowledge of oneself, and the true meaning of life. Also, children should learn that nothing happens without a reason and that everything is based on an accounting. Awareness of these spiritual principles strengthens children's self-esteem, provides them with stability in the face of life's difficulties, and safeguards them from committing irreparable mistakes during their adolescence and youth.

To help children absorb ethical and spiritual principles and not shun them when they reach adolescence, such principles should be taught in a pleasant and agreeable manner in the form of captivating and realistic stories that are appropriate for their age. More importantly, imposing difficult rituals and teaching principles in a dogmatic manner should be strictly avoided.

In general, the following points should be observed in educating children:

- Teaching and encouraging them to be truthful.

- Raising them to be independent at an early age and instilling within them a sense of responsibility, without placing unbearable pressure on them.

- Teaching them the true value of things: children should be grateful for the things they have and try to merit the things they want. For example, if they want something in particular they should be given a task whose performance would entitle them to it.

- Developing a sense of fiscal responsibility in children is one of the valuable elements of their education: they should learn how to spend, to avoid debt, and so forth.

- Teaching them to be neat and organized.

- Teaching them to be respectful toward others and to be polite and sociable.

- Keeping them away from unhealthy social relationships and instilling the necessary awareness to prevent them from being attracted to such things as smoking, drugs, etc., which are harmful and threaten their physical and psychological health. At the same time, they should not be supervised excessively.

- Not raising them in an overly spoiled or dependent manner. Likewise, they should not become accustomed to luxury or excessive comfort, for they will become satiated and will no longer be content with anything during their adulthood. Of course, deficiency in this regard is also wrong, for excessive deprivation can lead to complexes.

♦ Encouraging them to study, correctly guiding their innate curiosity, and directing their attention to the value of knowledge are extremely beneficial. Of course, one should be careful such encouragement does not exceed their capabilities and that their minds do not become tired. The brain is an organ like any other in the body and its excessive use, especially in the case of children, is detrimental. A brain that has become tired as a result of being overworked may become subject to neurosis or even psychosis, which in some cases may be irreparable.

♦ Encouraging them to observe the proper hygiene and health of their bodies, and especially to exercise.

♦ Helping them develop courage and perseverance.

♦ Teaching them other ethical virtues such as tolerance and mindfulness of others, and encouraging them to put these virtues into practice.

One of the important factors for success in the education and upbringing of children is the parents' awareness of their own behavior, especially in the case of mothers, since the smallest characteristics of the parents have deep effects on the child's emotional state. Because children instinctually understand their parents' psyche, parents have to be good role models and in particular ensure that their words and actions are in accord.[2] If parents actually practice the things they say, their children will usually do so as well.

The correct approach for making children receptive to what their parents are saying is to use psychological techniques rather than forcing them to do something through pressure, aggression, or fear. By bringing themselves down to the level of their child's understanding, parents can better explain things and help children until they are able to improve themselves. Severely reprimanding or physically punishing children shatters their personality; instead of criticizing them, especially in front of others, it is better if parents try to cultivate their personality and self-esteem until they themselves come to the realization that certain behaviors are beneath them. Establishing a sense of dignity in children is one of the primary pillars of a correct education.

When children become aware of their wrongdoing, they usually feel ashamed. In such a state, they do not like anyone to notice them and try to hide themselves. We should respect this feeling of shame and act as if we didn't see anything, while trying indirectly to make them understand they should not repeat that action. If they do repeat it, we should admonish and even threaten them so they become aware of the possible consequences of their action and realize it could lead to a punishment. At the same time, we should keep in mind that the more children are reproached, the less effect it will have. In contrast, each time they do something good, we should praise and encourage them. Usually, children who are treated with kindness will also be kind as adults.

Children by nature lack the faculty of discernment. At times, they desire to perform wrong actions, such as stealing or lying, and they are quite jealous (especially toward their siblings); they may also act as tattletales and liars. If we pay attention to these characteristics and guide them in the right direction, we can prevent them from becoming permanent attributes.

Finally, nothing is more destructive for a family than discriminating between children. Parents who discriminate between their children not only encounter familial problems, but must also account spiritually for their wrongdoing.

RELIGION

24. RELIGION

Religion is that which the Source taught human beings so they could come to know Him.

The Source is one, and His religion is also one. Likewise, all the divine envoys have received their knowledge from a unique Source. Divine religions complement one another, and the differences among them derive from human beings, who have taken secondary aspects for primary principles, the ephemeral for the enduring, and for one reason or another have altered the nature of religion.

It should be noted that the fundamental principles of the monotheistic religions are the same and can be summarized as follows:

- ◆ Belief in the existence of the unique Source.[1]

- ◆ Belief in eternal life and the final judgment (a spiritual accounting).

- ◆ Performing duties and observing rights.[2]

- ◆ The Source does not create "evil"—being evil is a consequence.

- ◆ Considering the world as an abode for developing one's celestial soul.

The Two Facets of Religion

Divine religions have two facets: an external or ritual facet (the level of exotericism), and an internal or spiritual facet (the level of esotericism). As such, the essence of religion is like the kernel of an almond enclosed by its shell.

Although the goal is to go beyond the shell and to reach the kernel, in the beginning we only see the shell without having any notion about the existence of the kernel. The main goal of all divine envoys is to make human beings aware of the spiritual aspect of religion, while the ritual aspect is intended as a preparatory stage for this next level.

The Level of Exotericism

At the exoteric level, human beings are concerned with the ritual aspect of religion and obedience. The goal of this level is to stabilize order and security in society and to prepare a believer to enter the level of esotericism or spirituality. The exoteric level consists in (1) fundamental principles, such as the uniqueness of the Creator, the day of judgment, etc. (2) ethical precepts, such as refraining from stealing, murdering, lying, etc., and (3) prescriptions, which are of two kinds: (a) social and customary prescriptions that oversee order, security, and material comfort, including a combination of social prescriptions relating to marriage, inheritance, transactions, etc.; and (b) devotional prescriptions that primarily consist in acts of devotion such as ritual prayers and fasting, offerings, alms, etc.

Acting on ethical precepts and prescriptions makes a believer more resistant to temptations and prevents him from committing vile acts. These prescriptions inevitably change according to the time, place, culture, intellectual development, and attitudes of human beings. The validity of any prescription during a specific time and under certain conditions does not necessarily mean it is applicable to another time and another set of conditions, which is why such prescriptions are called "secondary aspects" as opposed to fundamental principles, which do not change and are immutable.

At the exoteric level, the study of holy books is often limited to superficial inferences that usually serve as the source of contradictions and confusion, while at the spiritual level human beings are searching for deeper truths, and after finding such truths observe that there are no contradictions or differences among the principles of the celestial religions. In reality, limiting religion solely to its external aspect is one of the factors that lead to the manifestation of differences and prejudices among the various religions.

Faith in the fundamental principles of the divine religions and the practice of exoteric principles prepare the soul of a believer to ascend to the spiritual level. If a believer stops at the exoteric level, he will reach the paradise promised by the envoy of his religion, but if he manages to reach the spiritual level, he will be prepared for attaining the rank of perfection.

The Level of Esotericism (Spirituality)

Someone who has assimilated the ritual aspect of religion within his soul during this life or in past lives becomes thirsty for the truth. He asks himself, "What is the meaning of life? Where have I come from? Why am I here?" and other such questions. The superficial meaning of words no longer convinces him, and something deep within drives him to go beyond and to increase his knowledge of the Source. Such a state represents entry into the esoteric or spiritual level.

The esoteric level represents the culmination and continuation of the ritual level. The goal of this level is pure spirituality—that is, the search for truth, life in the next world, self-knowledge, and divine knowledge. The spiritual level draws all human beings closer together, whatever their religion may be, which is why in all ages there are true mystics present at the heart of every civilization and religious culture.[3] Having assimilated the essence of the exoteric level of religion within their souls, these mystics share a common language.[4]

The Goal of Religion

The main goal of religion is to teach us about the Source. In the age of the divine envoys, there were no better laws than the social laws of religion, which is why these envoys also set forth rules for daily life with the intention of establishing social justice, order, and security. Throughout the centuries, these rules—which had a completely social aspect to them—were added to the fundamental principles of religion; unfortunately, these rules gradually gained such importance that they overshadowed the main goal of religion, meaning its spiritual level.

If the secondary aspects of a divine religion are misrepresented, its spirit will still remain the same, but if its fundamental principles are subject to deviation, it will lose its soul. Once religion is deviated from its main purpose, it will take on more of a socio-economic form, and in such a state true believers will turn away from it over time, leading to a form of spiritual confusion for everyone. Moreover, as societies gradually evolve, the sense of civil and ethical responsibility for establishing social laws will suffice, without the need for religion to lower itself to the level of enacting social laws and preoccupying itself with such matters. More than anything else, today's human beings need the kind of spiritual truths that will answer their questions about the meaning of life and guide them toward self-knowledge and unicity.

The Religion of Man

When the ritual aspect of religion veils its spiritual aspect, divine religion declines in rank and is transformed into the "religion of man": opinions then abound, differences and dogmatic zealotries appear, and different denominations ultimately form, each denomination in turn breaking into various sects and branches. Consequently, chronic divisions and disputes are created among human beings. Normally, using religion for material goals in any form leads to its deviation. One of the signs of conversion from a divine religion to a manmade one is that its followers imagine it is only their denomination that will lead human beings to salvation. Such a mindset is not compatible with divine justice, for the Source exists everywhere.

False Religions

Alongside authentic religions, whose main message has more or less remained intact, there also exist false religions and denominations.[5] The founders of these denominations benefit from people's spiritual confusion and their lack of correct criteria, using their credulity as a tool to secure their own personal interests. Their traps are dangerous and even fatal for a soul that has yet to sufficiently develop.

The Creator will not allow anyone to be caught in the trap of false religions without sending warnings and signs: those who are enslaved by the whims of their imperious self interpret these signs according to their own desires. Those who truly seek the truth, however, will not be deceived by such temptations.

To distinguish between an authentic religion or divine spiritual path and a religion established at the hands of human beings, one has to sincerely ask the Source for help—without any prejudices or preconceptions—and analyze that religion with a sound mind while searching for the presence of any contradictions. A guide who does not have a direct connection with the Source tries to hide his ignorance by playing with words. If we pay attention, we will find many contradictions in the heart of his words, whereas a true spiritual path is devoid of contradictions and contains within it answers to all of the questions it raises.

25. The Evolutionary Stages of Religion

In every time and place, humankind ... has a pressing need for laws: in material affairs, laws that result in order and comfort in society, and in spiritual affairs, laws that lead to knowledge of oneself and the metacausal world.

Religion, too, is a creation, and like any other creation has its own process of perfection. The goal of religion is to guide human beings toward knowledge of the Source. All divine religions consist of four evolutionary stages: the first stage is the exoteric level, while the remaining three are related to the level of esotericism or spirituality.

The Level of Exotericism (Stage 1)

The exoteric level constitutes the first stage in the evolution of religion and corresponds to the material dimension or "external" aspect of religion. As such, one can enter this stage and benefit from it solely through faith. At this stage, a believer observes the prescriptions and rituals without seeking the reason or philosophy behind them and, by adhering to what has been prescribed and avoiding what has been proscribed, develops an inner sense of obedience and discipline. By teaching the rules of formal ritual prayers, basic ethics, the difference between good deeds and sins, and what is licit and illicit, the exoteric level serves as a preparatory stage for understanding the esoteric level. Once a believer assimilates within his soul the essence of the exoteric stage, acquires willpower and discipline with regard to his religion, and reaches an acceptable level of spiritual purity and maturity, the desire to understand the deeper meaning of that which he has put his faith in will automatically awaken within him. That is when he will naturally want to step foot onto the spiritual level and, to a certain extent, will sense the fragrance of truth within his own being.

The Level of Esotericism or Spirituality (Stages 2, 3, and 4)

The esoteric or spiritual level contains within it the essence of the teachings of all divine religions. At this level, content (meaning) is more relevant than form. Although there are various paths on the spiritual level, ultimately they all converge at a single point. In its traditional form, the spiritual level itself is divided into three stages: The Way, Knowledge, and Truth. The first two stages can be completed in any of the divine religions, notwithstanding that the prescriptions of a subsequent religion are more complete than those of its predecessor.

Even if a traveler at the stage of The Way senses differences between the methodologies of the various religions, in time he will discover at the stage of Knowledge that no such distinctions exist, and unity—which derives from Truth—will replace this sense of differentiation.

The stage of Truth constitutes the summit of the pyramid in the evolutionary stages of religions and the unique apex at which all religions converge. Regardless of their path or religion, those who enter the stages of Knowledge and Truth all reach unity at the level of "unicity"—they understand spiritual truths and act upon divine prescriptions in the same manner, developing the same attributes and the same ethical and spiritual values within themselves.

The Way (Stage 2)

In the second evolutionary stage of religion, a traveler enters the realm of becoming familiar with and fighting against his imperious self. In addition to the orders and prescriptions of the exoteric level, he also observes more precise orders at this stage so he can better know his imperious self and better fight against its illicit impulses and desires. There is no contradiction between these additional prescriptions and the fundamental principles of the exoteric level. At the end of this stage, a traveler reaches a state of purity and detachment, which we could call a celestial state. He becomes detached from worldly interests and material temptations, and his carnal whims and desires subside.

Knowledge (Stage 3)

In the third stage, a traveler develops an understanding of his self, meaning he comes to know his own self and, to the same extent, the Source. His faith transforms into certitude, and he becomes aware of the absolute power and immensity of the Source. At the culmination of this stage, he gains control over his terrestrial desires and innately despises actions that are beneath the dignity of his soul.

Truth (Stage 4)

In the fourth stage of the evolution of religion, a traveler spiritually joins the Source of Truth. This stage is based on (1) renewing the primordial covenant of human beings with the Source (2) knowing the manifestation of the Source, and (3) understanding the principle of successive lives.

The practical prescriptions at the stage of Truth are based on four virtues: purity, rectitude, self-effacement, and self-abnegation.

* *Purity* in its broadest sense encompasses all aspects of one's life: purity in a material sense (cleanliness of one's home, clothing, body, etc.) and in a

spiritual sense (a licit livelihood, pure thoughts, pure speech, pure deeds, etc.).

• *Rectitude* is to travel the path that directly leads to the Source, meaning to devote oneself to Him, to be loyal to Him, to be resigned to His will, to act upon his prescriptions, and to refrain from all forms of malevolence and lying.

• *Self-Effacement* consists in eliminating pride, selfishness, self-centeredness, excesses of the imperious self, and all base and undignified characteristics. Once we can control all of these vices, we innately become resigned to His will and desire only His satisfaction.

• *Self-Abnegation* means to assist and help others to the extent of being a refuge for them, and to want and act upon what is good for them without any self-interest. Self-abnegation in the spiritual context also means contentedness in the specific sense—that is, to reach a level where one's will becomes the divine will.

With the exception of their close companions, none of the divine saints in the past revealed this fourth stage to the public, for its time had yet to come. For example, Christ only revealed it to his disciples, while Ali revealed it solely to his closest companions. Although more people today are gaining access to this stage, it is still concealed among three layers (Exotericism, The Way, and Knowledge) and to reach it requires that one spiritually complete the preceding stages.

After the stage of Truth, three more levels exist before reaching perfection. No being is capable of completing these three levels on his own, and it is only the Source that selects whomever He wishes.

Each of the four stages of religion has its own specific laws, orders, and prescriptions, all of which appear one after the other along a continuum. In *natural spirituality*, however, it is possible to traverse these four stages simultaneously.

26. MIRACLES

A miracle is a divine phenomenon, the likes of which human beings are unable to perform.

The purpose of miracles is to attract the attention of human beings toward the Source. The miracles of the divine envoys are phenomena that are realized without any tools or advance preparation—accomplished solely by divine will and authorization—and in every era the people of that time are unable to perform them. Though it is possible that such phenomena may later be reconstructed with the help of science or certain paranormal methods, in these cases they can no longer be considered miracles.

The Miracle of the Envoys

Miracles are a testament to the authenticity of the mission of divine envoys and thus constitute a sign for people to recognize who they are; that is why every true religion must be accompanied by miracles.

Another benefit of miracles is that they give human beings confidence in the existence of another world and a higher power, thus encouraging people to go toward that higher power. Miracles leave a deep impact provided that they transcend a domain in which the people of that era have attained maximum proficiency. In the time of Moses, for example, the realm of magic and sorcery had reached its pinnacle; in the time of Muhammad, the art of speech and eloquence had reached its zenith. Miracles, then, are a "divine argument" and are always inexplicable by the laws of nature—neither science nor sorcery can match them.

In general, those who are assigned the mission of guidance by the Source bear some kind of miracle.

Other Miracles

If a group of united believers with a common goal focuses on the Source, they can actually perform a miracle: just as the accumulated force resulting from water drops that have frozen together can split a boulder, the joining and accumulation of particles originating from the divine breath in human beings can attract divine energy and accomplish a miracle. It is such phenomena that are at times clearly manifest in certain pilgrimage sites.

Prodigies

It is necessary to differentiate between miracles and prodigies—which sometimes appear as miracles—and to analyze their sources and motivations, for many mental deviations stem from the inability to distinguish between the two. The source of miracles is the spiritual world, whereas prodigies result from a form of expertise and lengthy training that enables the use of certain energies. Overall, there are two main sources of prodigies (1) the psychosomatic organism of human beings, which is a reservoir of potential energies, and (2) the energy of a group of negative spirits, which some people can manipulate to help them achieve their material goals. Consequently, as a result of lengthy practices and the use of specific techniques (asceticism, meditation, occult sciences, etc.), anyone can perform prodigies, including reading thoughts, making objects appear, levitating, and passing through matter. Such phenomena belong to the category of paranormal powers, not miracles.

Unlike miracles, then, prodigies are explicable on the basis of the laws of nature, even if science cannot currently explain them. In addition, miracles are realized without any material self-interest and only with divine authorization, whereas prodigies are often performed with the intention of displaying power, being admired and praised by others, etc.

Wonders

Wonders, like miracles, are divine phenomena, meaning they transcend the laws of nature. Unlike miracles, however, wonders are not obtained for "free"—the divine system gives them to those who request them.[1] If an individual's request is accepted, an equivalent sum will be deducted from his spiritual reserves. Each person is free to spend his spiritual reserves however he likes: some use it to buy wonders or to access mystical secrets, others to secure a place in heaven. The wisest course is to not touch one's spiritual reserves and to leave them with Him, and to want nothing but divine satisfaction.

The Miracle of our Time

The time for the miracles of the great envoys, which were intended to be public and to have an impact on the masses, has come to an end. The culture and mentality of people have changed, and the overt miracles of the past no longer cause people today to collectively have faith, let alone to persuade them to actively take a step on the divine path. Human beings today rely more on reason than emotion, and need to understand to be convinced.

Considering human beings are the intended recipients of miracles and that their attitudes change with the passage of time, miracles must also be in accordance with the times. In our era, miracles are revealed through *rationality* and *divine impact*. For example, spirituality should be so logical and coherent as to contain within it rational and convincing answers to the questions that it raises. Divine impact is the transcendent quality concealed within guidance that causes guidance to touch a person's heart. Someone who bears the divine impact in his being and words can, if he wishes, awaken faith in people's hearts through his presence, his regard, or his words.[2] Faith is a heartfelt emotion that cannot be negated, explained, or imitated. If someone today doubts the existence of the Source or even denies Him, and solely by hearing some words about Him develops faith and diligently decides to act upon his faith without being promised the slightest material gain, that is a miracle. And the goal and essence of a miracle is none other than to permeate the heart and awaken the soul.

27. THE DIVINE ENVOYS

When you view all the envoys and saints as True and no longer differentiate between religions, you have entered the realm of mysticism.

S omeone whose celestial soul is healthy is thirsty for the truth: he is searching for answers to life's fundamental questions and is seeking the "truth" in all circumstances. To respond to this state, the divine envoys have left behind all that is necessary. Among them, some had the mission of founding a religion and provided their followers with a book. Although the writings or sayings attributed to them are available, determining the authenticity of what remains and understanding their real meaning requires an awake and educated soul, for material education alone is insufficient in this regard. If we could investigate the *authentic* messages of the great divine envoys, we would realize that they all derive from the same source.

Among the many envoys who bore the divine message, we will refer to five who brought forth a book.

Moses

The Source chose Moses to free the Israelites from bondage, to guide them to the Promised Land, and to give them a nation, a religion, and exoteric laws. It was Moses who united the different tribes of Israel into a single tribe under the banner of Yahweh. The Ten Commandments were revealed to him from the Source, and he performed numerous miracles. For example, whenever he willed it, he shone a light from his hand, or turned his staff into a serpent. None of the malevolent individuals or those who denied him were capable of matching his miracles. After lengthy preparations, the

Pharaoh's sorcerers were able to materialize snakes, but Moses' snake consumed them all; the sorcerers were disarmed before Moses' power, which derived from God. They ultimately had no choice but to acknowledge the enormous difference between their sorcery and Moses' divine power, and some of them thus accepted Moses' God.

Among the other Jewish prophets, we can name David, the second king of the Hebrews, whose Psalms are famous, as well as Solomon, David's son and successor, who built the temple in Jerusalem and to whom the Source granted the knowledge of ascertaining truths. Daniel was chosen to be a prophet because of his patience and persistence during his exile, and his predictions have been subject to less tampering than those of the other Israelite prophets.

Zoroaster

Zoroaster was an envoy with a universal mission. Although selected from the time he was a child, he only gradually revealed his mission. He received revelations, and his teachings have been collected in a book called "Avesta," whose original has since disappeared. Zoroaster was a monotheist, and taught that there were two opposing forces in the universe: good (AhuraMazda) and evil (Ahriman). He believed in the concept of multiple lives and refers in his sayings to a constant inner struggle within human beings between AhuraMazda (the soul) and Ahriman (the imperious self). Zoroaster considered the goal of human beings to be a constant struggle for good to completely overcome evil, and analogized the spiritual illuminations he experienced to the radiance of fire, which is why some have considered him to worship fire. His motto was "good thoughts, good deeds, and good words."

Buddha

Like Zoroaster, Buddha was an envoy with a universal mission. Appointed from childhood, he revealed himself gradually to the people. Although he used to delve within and receive revelations from the time he was a young boy, the manuscript containing these revelations no longer exists. Buddha accepted the cycle of multiple lives and viewed everything in this world as suffering. The life of human beings is all suffering, and the source of this suffering stems from the desires of their imperious self and their ignorance. He revealed the process of perfection to people step by step, and believed human beings should eliminate their desires through their internal forces in order to release themselves from the cycle of re-births and reach nirvana (liberation, absolute bliss, etc.). When asked about the other world, he replied: "You will understand once you arrive there;" concealed in this statement is a profound meaning. Unfortunately, as is the case with the other envoys, a large part of what is attributed to Buddha is not from him.

Jesus

Jesus Christ was an envoy with a universal mission. He was the bearer of revelation—he came to the world perfect and had the mission of saving humanity. Christ's teachings are mostly concerned with undertaking the spiritual levels of religion: the existence of the soul, returning to the Source, eternal life, etc. A large part of his teachings has been lost, while the sayings that have been preserved over time are often presented outside of their original context and thus have not been properly understood. Jesus Christ performed many miracles: he was a physician of the soul as well as a healer of the body. To test him and to ensure the authenticity of his miracles, his detractors chose impossible challenges: bringing the dead to life, breathing life into a clay bird, giving sight to those who were born blind, healing incurable illnesses, etc. His miracles were real. Without divine authorization and power, no one is able to bring the dead back to life and return a soul to a body from which it has already departed. Science will never be able to revive someone who has *truly* died, for when the cord between the celestial soul and the material body is severed, it is impossible for life to return.[1] Neither nature nor science is able to change the direction of this current—only the divine will is capable of restoring life.

Muhammad

Muhammad's mission was also universal. In an age when the Arabic language and the art of eloquence had reached their zenith, he brought forth the Koran (despite his illiteracy), which even from the standpoint of its outward form has been recognized as the most distinguished masterpiece of the Arabic language.

For the oppositionists of Muhammad's time, the miracle of the Koran was the sign of an indisputable and undeniable divine argument.[2] No effect was able to rival the Koran, and to date no one has been able to produce a single sura (chapter) like it. In addition to the rank of prophecy, he was an honest, just, and kind human being who manifested ethical virtues. Although an advocate of peace, when he received the divine command for a holy war to preserve religion, he did not abandon his responsibility.[3]

The fundamental principles of the envoys' teachings do not contradict one another, and none of them have negated their predecessors. From the time of Adam to the present, all the divine envoys have communicated the same authentic and fundamental principles of religion. Unfortunately, over time and in the course of transmission from one generation to the next, they have inevitably taken on a human color and have become subject to adaptations and even deviations, which is why they have gradually diminished in clarity and transparency and have become distanced from their original content. Despite the fact that these principles are always the same, their application in different periods and different cultures must be in accordance with the times. Consequently, the Source designates an emissary in each period to remind human beings, on the one hand, of divine principles that have been forgotten, tarnished over time, or altered by human beings, and on the other hand to teach new complementary principles that answer the necessities of that era.

The Advent of the Messiah

All of the monotheistic religions are awaiting the arrival or manifestation of the messiah (Savior) and are of the belief that following such manifestation, justice and peace will prevail on earth. According to the conviction of these religions, the Savior will be one of the envoys or saints from within that religion.[4]

In reality, the messiah of all the religions is one unique essence (Savior), which in addition to guidance will also have the mission to prove this universal event to all of humanity in due time.[5] By the grace of his presence on earth, injustice and lying will be eliminated through science, and the right of each person will be respected, as each will receive what he deserves. Science will prove the existence of the Source and the validity of certain spiritual laws, and it is then that disputes and fanaticism among the religions will come to an end. Only one spirituality will remain, and that will be the true spirituality whose authenticity everyone will certify, though each person will be free to practice it or not.

Although everyone will benefit from the generosity of the manifestation of this messiah, we should not expect that everyone will personally know him. Just as the Source is present everywhere but only the spiritually awake see Him, the messiah will also be recognized by those who have reached a sufficient level of spiritual growth.

Considering that the exact time of this event is unknown to everyone and various interpretations—and even contradictions—exist in this regard, it is reasonable for human beings to make an effort to know the Truth and its manifestations in every time, in which case the manifestation of the Savior becomes a current reality, for His **Vali** or representative is always present on earth.

28. THE SPIRITUAL HIERARCHY

The earth is never devoid of a divine representative.

To avoid being bewildered in the pursuit of spirituality, human beings have to consciously choose the direction of their thought and recognize which mindset is most beneficial to them. To find the right direction, to know whom to listen to, and to be able to confidently travel the path toward the Source, it is necessary to some extent to know the hierarchy of spiritual levels. As examining the details of this hierarchy is beyond the scope of this book, we will discuss only a few of its main aspects here.

The Total Soul

At the outset, the Source created the **Total Soul** (**Quiddity**) and made it the cause of all beings, which gradually came into existence.[1] The relation of the Total Soul to the Source is like the relation of attribute to essence: the Total Soul can be considered the form in which the Source manifests to make itself known to beings of the material world, including humankind. The essence of the Source is unknowable, even for those who have attained perfection. Only the Source and the Total Soul, which is not outside of Him, are aware of this essence. In reality, when we speak of the Source, we are referring to this Supreme Being (Total Soul)—what lies beyond Him cannot be fathomed by the imagination of any being. The Total Soul has come into existence from divine thought and consequently encompasses the entire universe, reflecting divine thought and power.

The Saviors

From the Total Soul, a few souls of the highest level called **Saviors** were created.[2] Endowed with the "divine regard," they are superior to all beings and are responsible for divine missions (including the guidance of beings).[3] In compliance with divine justice, these superior souls descend on the planets and enter material bodies to guide beings toward their source. On earth, these exalted souls appear in the form of human beings so that like other humans, they can undergo their spiritual process of perfection in a material body. They mostly present themselves to others as envoys, saints, sacred men and women, etc.

Each of these Saviors can manifest on earth in a body of its own, or it can reflect the light of its essence for a certain period of time (from a few moments to an entire lifetime) in a man or woman who has acquired the worthiness to accomplish its will. This radiance may be limited to a weak ray or to its entire light.

In every age, there is always a large group of individuals who imitate the external appearance of these exalted figures in order to attract people and fulfill their own material interests. Such individuals bear a negative force, sometimes without even knowing it, and pull those who follow them into an abyss in which they themselves belong.

Knowing the spiritual hierarchy helps us to think and choose correctly before selecting a guide or adhering to a spiritual path.

The Vali

From the beginning of humankind, there has always been an individual on earth with the rank of the divine representative who reflects the light of the divine essence; such an individual is called the *Vali*. He is the spiritual pole entrusted with divine power and thought on earth. In reality, the Vali is one of the Saviors. By studying the lives of some of the divine representatives, we can form an image of what the Vali can be like.

From time to time, an exceptional event takes place: the Total Soul manifests in a material body. At that point, the Vali is no longer one of the Saviors, but rather the manifestation of the divine essence. It is in such conditions that the concept of the **Absolute Vali** arises. The Absolute Vali is the manifestation of the essence, thought, and power of the Source, not only on earth but possibly for the entire universe.

In each period, the last Absolute Vali that has come to earth is called the Divinity of the Time.[4] The Divinity of the Time is the form in which human beings can and should come to know the Source if they seek perfection. Throughout the history of humankind, many *Valis* have appeared, but the manifestation of the Absolute Vali has been rare, and only three of them have been Absolute Valis in the true sense of the word.[5] The last time the divine essence manifested in its totality on earth was also its final manifestation.

The rank of the Vali has always existed and will continue to exist until the end of humanity. As soon as the Vali leaves this world, another Vali is appointed by the Source to replace him. Some Valis have also been envoys, but most of them have lived a simple life away from fame, making themselves known to only a few.

Under the supervision of the Vali, there are guides and more or less advanced spiritual teachers everywhere who can show seekers the path and guide them to the level they themselves occupy.[6] If they are authentic, they make no claims as such, their behavior is simple and natural, and their lifestyle is in harmony with the time and social environment in which they live. These guides are present throughout the world, among all societies, cultures, and nations; spiritually linked to the Vali, they receive their light from him, even if they are unaware of it themselves. The "light" from the Source that comes to the earth passes through the Vali's being, and each person can benefit from its reflection to the extent of his merit.

SPIRITUAL COMMUNICATION

- ❖ Prayer and Meditation

- ❖ Music

- ❖ Dreams

- ❖ Communicating with Souls

- ❖ Other Beings

29. PRAYER AND MEDITATION

If we envision Him as face-to-face with us while praying, we would not speak to Him inattentively.

Human beings, even those with faith, tend to forget the Source unless they are in situations of need or distress. The goal of prayer is to prevent this forgetfulness and to maintain our communication with the Source. Prayer turns a believer's "receptor" toward the Source and in doing so enables him to receive divine energy, which is a panacea for all ills, especially illnesses of the soul.[1] This energy keeps the soul lively, purifying it, increasing its radiance and, most importantly, preventing its negligence and ignorance.

The Conditions of Prayer

The main factor in prayer is heartfelt attention. True prayer is one that is performed solely with the intention of drawing closer to the Source and being mindful of His presence. According to this principle, then, what is important is "attention," which supersedes words.

When we pray, it is as if our prayer is recorded on a magnetic tape. If what we recite within is done with attention and its meaning resonates in our mind, it will be recorded in its entirety. Conversely, any moments of inattention also remain on the tape in the form of blank spaces, as if no prayer were ever recited. In general, if prayer is performed without attention, no message will be sent, in which case the only reward we receive is for the physical effort we've imposed on ourselves to recite the prayer.

When performed with heartfelt attention, prayer in any form will reach the Source; if it is accompanied by a sense of excitement as well, it will have an even greater effect. Such excitement can be engendered by music, joyous songs, a specific environment, etc.[2] The greater the enthusiasm and fervor, the more excited the heart becomes and the more the prayer increases in effect. If we invoke the Source in difficult situations with the same anguish and heart-felt excitement as that of a person stranded in the middle of the ocean on a sinking boat, He will respond to us.

What we want from the Source through our prayers depends on our culture, upbringing, and spiritual level. Someone who is spiritually at the exoteric level may have both material and spiritual desires. Having material desires at this level does not matter and can even be beneficial, meaning we can come to better know the Source in this manner and establish a closer relationship with Him. At the level of esotericism or spirituality, however, an individual's nature changes and with it his needs, such that he no longer has any material desires. In this state, he wishes to love the Source more and draw closer to Him, seeking above all else divine satisfaction. He asks the Source to protect him from the rebellions of his imperious self and to grant him the grace to remain steadfast on his path.

Regardless of our spiritual level, one of our duties is to ask for "forgiveness, mercy, blessings, and grace for the souls of our parents (whether alive or deceased), all the men and women of faith, and even for all of creation." If a person asks us to pray for him or for a third person, we can do so provided we leave its result to "whatever the Source deems expedient."

Above all, then, prayer is a means of communicating with the Source and receiving energy from Him.

The Stages of Prayer

Prayer has four stages, each of which corresponds to one of the four stages of religion (Exotericism, The Way, Knowledge, and Truth).[3] The transformations that occur in a person's inner self during

162

prayer are indicative of his spiritual level and stage. The first stage relates to exoteric prayers, while the next three correspond to spiritual (mystical) states.

The first stage of prayer corresponds to the exoteric level. At this stage, there is a physical and obeisant aspect to prayer, which is performed in the form of specific words with the intention of fulfilling one's exoteric duty. The believer repeats designated phrases (words have only a formal and literal meaning to him) and makes an effort to focus his mind on the Source and not to allow his attention to be diverted. If someone performs his exoteric and ethical duties correctly, it will have the effect of protecting him from committing vile acts and will prepare his soul for entering higher spiritual levels. Performing exoteric prayers is similar to announcing one's presence at a roll call. Although this form of prayer does not always result in a heartfelt connection, it is considered a preparatory stage for such a connection.

The second stage of prayer corresponds to The Way. The person's consciousness expands beyond his mind and reaches his heart, resulting in a celestial state. In this stage, prayer originates from the heart, as if the person is attracted by the magnetism of the Source.[4] Becoming detached from whimsical desires, physical attachments, and material attractions, he no longer has to struggle against distracting thoughts to focus his attention on the Source. Words slowly begin to take on a truer and more profound meaning, influencing his whole being. He sees himself in the realm of divine grace, in the vicinity of the celestial world, and in the shadow of the Source. This state marks the beginning of spiritual awakening.

The third stage of prayer corresponds to Knowledge. Here, prayer transcends the level of the heart and ascends to the level of the celestial soul. Free from the body, the person gains access to a world whose attractions and wonders are beyond imagination. The feeling of divine power and omnipotence arises within him, and he becomes conscious of his inner self. Those who reach this level develop confidence about the truth of their faith, and from faith reach the level of certitude.

The fourth stage of prayer corresponds to the stage of Truth. The person's soul has joined the realm of Truth, meaning proximity to the infinite Source. Someone who reaches this level is so immersed in bliss, joy, and wonder that he forgets his self and with lighthearted elation plunges into the ocean of unicity: his soul has joined the Truth.

Natural Meditation

Natural Meditation involves making an effort not to see ourselves as alone in the midst of daily life and to feel the Source present and observant at all times.[5] This does not require achieving a particular physical state or performing any physical exercises or specific techniques. At the beginning, it is sufficient to try to envision His presence beside us, observing us at all times, and to believe that He is always with us in order to help us, while trying to have the intention of attracting His satisfaction in the decisions that we make.

For this mental effort to be more effective and to lead to quicker results, it is necessary to devise and regularly practice a structured program of prayer, trying to recite the words with presence of mind throughout the prayer.[6] After some time, this state of natural meditation will be transformed into part of our nature,[7] and we will naturally act in accordance with divine satisfaction: from that point on, all of our actions, thoughts, and words become like a prayer.[8] With such a mindset, we can say that someone who helps a needy person; responsible parents who work hard to help their child understand faith and ethical qualities; a physician who treats patients conscientiously; a student who studies with the intention of serving his community and being a beneficial member of society; an honest judge who does not succumb to pressures and temptations—all are in a state of prayer, provided they act in accordance with the voice of their conscience or to attract divine satisfaction, even if they appear preoccupied with carrying out their daily activities. Each of them, at his own level, is in a state of natural meditation, for the voice of the conscience originates from the Source, and listening to one's conscience is to unite oneself with the Source, whether one believes in this principle or not.

The benefit of natural meditation is that we gradually develop divine virtues and consequently become more at peace with ourselves. We automatically enjoy greater inner serenity and the difficulties of life upset us less; in short, we feel greater reliance, confidence, hope, and prosperity. Each time we focus our attention on the Source, we have positioned ourselves to receive His light, and the energy of such light is necessary for the growth and development of the soul.

30. Music

Music is related to the soul and the soul is related to the Source—pity it has mainly been turned into a vehicle for material pleasure.

Beyond its technical dimensions and artistic applications, music is a language for the soul, an art that exists in various forms at all levels of creation. In the beginning, music was created to stimulate spiritual emotions, for it is endowed with the quality of being able to directly affect the heart and animate the celestial soul, thereby facilitating communication with the Source.

The soul is inherently in love with "celestial music." It is said that when Adam's body was created it remained without a celestial soul for quite some time, since the soul had an aversion to entering it. It was not until a group of archangels entered Adam's body and began to play music that the soul was overcome with excitement and ecstasy, thus entering the body.

Like any other created being, music has its own specific properties and effects, many of which remain unknown. Every being endowed with a soul is sensitive to music, which has interesting effects on all things, even plants and minerals. Certain songs, for example, have therapeutic effects, others help to focus the mind, and still others like military marches have a special power that can galvanize a combatant spirit.[1]

The main effect of music is to influence the soul through the affective and emotional centers. Thus, rhythmical prayers accompanied by the appropriate songs excite the celestial soul and consequently facilitate communication with the Source. As a result of the intensity of the excitement, an individual may enter a state of ecstasy, lose himself in rapture, and even experience visions and inspirations.

Within the "particles" of music—for those able to see or sense them—there is a special latent energy that sometimes takes form and manifests as scenes that were in the thoughts and intentions of the composer at the time the music was created.[2] If the thoughts and intentions of the composer were spiritual, the scenes will also be spiritual; if they were material and carnal, the scenes will reflect the same.

The effects emanating from music, therefore, are a specific reflection of the composer, but are dependent on other factors as well, such as the performer, the listener, the environment, the musical instrument, and the melody.

- ♦ *The artist*: the composer (and to a lesser extent, the performer) is the most important factor in the effect that music bears. The effect of music relates to the quality and state of the artist, which stem from his intention.[3] The intention transcends the effects of technical skills and aesthetic aspects, imparting the melody with a soul and determining its value and importance. Accordingly, a melody composed with the intention of stimulating sensual emotions will have no effect on the celestial soul and may even cause it to feel sluggish, for the energy emanating from it awakens and strengthens the id. Likewise, it is the intention of the artist that differentiates spiritual music from non-spiritual music, regardless of the actual genre of the music. As such, it is possible for a religious song to have no spiritual effect and for a so-called popular song to emanate spiritual effects. Having a positive intention while composing and performing a song establishes a form of contact or communication with the Source. Hence, a performer who succeeds in delving within and focusing his attention on the Source can receive inspiration from the spiritual world and elevate his music to its true dimension. The purer and more spiritual the intention, the more useful and effective the positive energy that derives from it.[4] The relation between an artist and his music is like the relation between a flower and its fragrance: music derives its soul from the artist, just as perfume derives its fragrance from a flower.

♦ *The listener*: the effect of music also depends upon the cultural background and psychospiritual state of the listener. One must consider the person's cultural background, the sort of music with which he is familiar, the kind of feelings he has, his state of being while listening, etc. These factors result in creating different reactions to the same song. For example, the same song may cause some individuals to want to dance, others to recall happy memories, and still others to recall separation or loss of loved ones, making them sad. In some people, it can even cause such feelings of joy or spiritual nostalgia that they weep or enter into states of ecstasy.

Between the composer, performer, and listener, it is the composer who determines the quality of the music, although the performer and listener can also have an effect on the quality and alter the nature of the music's energy. That is why listeners can neutralize the effects of the negative energy of sensual songs on themselves with a spiritual intention and vice versa. On the other hand, if the creator (the composer) has an exalted spiritual rank (one of the Saviors, for example), one cannot easily change the positive energy of his music nor the scenes that emanate from it.

♦ *The environment or ambiance*: the ambiance is contingent on the location, the sociocultural background, the time (each period during the day and night is suitable for a particular song), and the conditions under which the music is performed (a concert, prayer, etc.). Each of these factors leaves a particular effect on the artist and the listener.

- *The means of creating the melody*: the human voice, musical instruments, the songs and sonorities of animals and birds, the sounds of nature (the blowing of wind, the flow of a spring), etc. The most beautiful melodies—for those who are capable of hearing or "seeing" them—are the murmuring sounds of nature and the melodies of the world above.[5]

- *Melodies*: sounds, intervals, and beats. It is the manner in which these elements are arranged that causes music to have a greater or lesser effect on the affective centers, to excite the soul, to stimulate emotions (sorrow, joy, courage, ecstasy, etc.), or to engender therapeutic effects. For example, the wavelength of certain melodies or intervals is in harmony with that of the melodies of the spiritual world and thus causes a more intense attraction in the celestial soul.

31. DREAMS

Dreams are one of the strong reasons—even a definitive argument—for proving the existence of the soul.

One of the means of communicating with the spiritual world is through dreams.[1] When we are awake, the activity of our psychological system (mind) creates a dense and dark veil that prevents the transfer of the celestial soul's perceptions to our ordinary level of consciousness.[2] This veil normally becomes penetrable during sleep, and in some instances is completely removed, thereby increasing the possibility of having spiritual dreams. As long as this dense psychological veil remains, however, spiritual transmissions will be blocked, and our dreams will merely be the reflection of daily events or impulses of the unconscious, which we call *cerebral dreams.*

Different Kinds of Dreams

To simplify the subject, dreams can generally be divided into three main categories: cerebral dreams, spiritual dreams, and mixed dreams.

Almost all of the dreams of those under the control of their terrestrial soul (id) are cerebral dreams. Although contact with the spiritual world is established during sleep, the density of the psychological veil prevents the reception of messages. Cerebral dreams arise from daily events, repressed impulses, and psychological tendencies, and their content depends upon one's physical and psychological state or the events in one's life. Another factor for distinguishing cerebral dreams from spiritual ones is that they do not often leave a deep and lasting effect on the individual.

Spiritual dreams can be distinguished by their quality, content, and effect on the dreamer. In such dreams, which often contain coded messages, an envoy from the spiritual world usually contacts the dreamer, or the soul of the dreamer leaves its body and establishes contact with the other world; in the latter case, the soul is connected to the body by a "cord" that sustains the body's life. Spiritual dreams also leave a profound effect: if we do not forget them upon waking up, when we do recall them—even years later—we will still find them to be fresh in our minds.

We usually forget part or all of our spiritual dreams upon waking up. This is due to the fact that we either have yet to acquire sufficient spiritual maturity, it is not in our best interest, or the soul's negligence prevents the recording of our dreams. In reality, the negligence of the soul causes the connection to be lost at the moment of transmission to the conscious. To prevent such negligence, it has been recommended to have attention to the Source before going to sleep.

Most dreams are of the mixed kind, meaning that psychological elements are dominant within them.

The Meaning of Dreams

The content and scenes of spiritual dreams depend on an individual's culture, social environment, and in particular the nature of his beliefs. For example, if someone dreams of a saint or prophet, he will see that saint or prophet with the appearance and characteristics preconceived in his mind, which may not correspond to that saint's actual characteristics.[3] As such, each person usually sees his spiritual messages in the form of codes or symbols that have a specific meaning for him. That is why only spiritually lucid interpreters familiar with the language and implications of the spiritual world can correctly decode and interpret spiritual dreams. These interpreters can see the spiritual currents that have created a particular scene. Imagine, for example, that a play is going on under several spotlights and the shadows of the characters are cast on the wall. A lucid interpreter can see all of those scenes and activities as they actually are, whereas ordinary interpreters of dreams, meaning those who interpret dreams based on conventional symbolism, see only the shadows of the characters cast on the wall.

Interpreters can have an effect—positive or negative—on the consequences of a dream. For example, if someone has a dream and another person interprets it in a negative way, there is a strong likelihood that this negative interpretation will materialize. Lucid interpreters are capable of changing the negative effects of a dream and even turning them into positive outcomes through their positive interpretations. If such an interpreter is not available, however, each person can interpret his own dream better than others.

Sometimes spiritual dreams have such a clear and evident meaning there is no need for interpretation. For example, a clear instruction is given, a recommendation is made, or something is clearly prescribed to us. The gauge for determining whether to act on such dreams is to see if their message adheres to the following three criteria: a sound mind, divine laws, and ethical principles.

Worrisome Premonitory Dreams

For some reason—such as our past, for example—an unpleasant incident may be recorded in our variable destiny.[4] At the same time, we may also have acquired spiritual points later on that merit the attention of the Source. Under these circumstances, justice would no longer necessitate such an unpleasant incident from occurring. By having a frightening or unpleasant dream, therefore, we are given a warning so that we can prevent this incident from taking place. In such cases, we can reduce the severity of the incident or even eliminate it by pleading to the Source (prayer, offerings, alms) in accordance with our own culture and beliefs, and it is more effective if we do so at the first available opportunity after awakening.

If we have a frightening dream about someone close to us, we can personally make an offering for that person, provided that the dream is related to one of our close family members (child, spouse, parent, etc.). In the case of dreams about other individuals, if we know that our dream will be taken seriously, we can relay it to them.

On the other hand, a sound mind dictates that we should not act upon all dreams, including the dreams of children, the frightening and repetitive dreams of mothers worried about their children, or worrisome dreams about those who are dear to us.

Cerebral dreams hold a special place in psychology, for most contain signs from which it is possible to diagnose certain symptoms of neurosis and psychosis.

32. COMMUNICATING WITH SOULS

The essence of existence is the soul; the body is merely a tool for our being, not being itself.

It sometimes happens that the deceased want to contact us to relay a message, express a request, visit close ones, or perform a mission. If granted permission, these souls can make their presence known in different ways. Before a soul manifests itself, it usually signals its arrival in some form, which we experience as a certain state (excitement, a sensation, etc.). Souls can announce their presence by creating sounds (whispering, breathing, murmuring, speaking) or emitting odors, or make themselves perceivable in some other way; in rare instances, they can make themselves palpable. Depending on their spiritual rank, the deceased can manifest themselves in one or several or even all of their earthly bodies. Most, however, present themselves in the form of their last body. High-ranking spiritual figures have no limitations as to their appearance: the vibratory frequency of their being can manifest in any form and in any physical density they choose.

If granted permission, the spiritually impoverished (i.e., impoverished souls)—those who have done nothing for their future life while living in the material world—or those who seek forgiveness for their undignified acts, can contact the living to request help. It is possible to help the spiritually impoverished by performing charitable deeds such as offerings, alms, etc., and to donate their spiritual reward to them. As for the second group making contact to seek forgiveness, they have found their salvation in the forgiveness of the wronged person. Apart from these cases, there are also wandering souls that have yet to receive permission to enter the interworld—we can help this group as well by performing charitable deeds on their behalf such as offerings and alms.

In general, we should not fear souls of the deceased, for in principle they have a celestial nature. It has even been recommended that we look upon them with respect and help them with charitable prayers—such acts result in their happiness. Even if souls have a bad intention, they will not be allowed to contact someone on their own volition. Things that normally appear in frightening forms are often the result of our own imagination, or our negative actions embodied in this manner to penalize and reform us. In addition, such souls can also be a part of the group of negative "vicious" spirits; these souls are not of the same kind as human souls.[1]

Communicating with souls through séances, meditation, or other means is a different matter. If the goal behind such acts is to acquire information about the truths of the spiritual world, one should consider that these deceased individuals do not know everything and their information corresponds only to their spiritual level. The knowledge of most souls does not exceed that which they acquired during their own lives on earth. Moreover, even if a soul knows something about the spiritual world, it may not have permission to divulge it. Souls can often convey only unimportant and incomplete information. On the other hand, there are also souls with a mischievous temperament who relay messages that confuse us without lying. Therefore, it is better to ask souls to relay their messages clearly and without ambiguity, and to put aside any matters that do not conform to divine principles and a sound mind.

In general, contacting the deceased through séances is ominous, especially if the goal is recreation or to discover secretive information about this world. Souls generally do not like to be asked anything about material affairs. Summoning souls through a séance may be acceptable in certain specific cases: for example, when it is done to strengthen one's faith, or for a scientific purpose such as proving the existence of the soul or life after death.

Conversely, establishing contact with great spiritual figures (authentic divine envoys and saints) by recalling them during prayer, pleading to them, going on pilgrimages, etc., is a source of grace and blessing.

33. OTHER BEINGS

> *The same Source that created angels, human beings, animals, plants, and minerals has also created other beings. Each has its own specific reason for existence, receiving and in turn providing some benefit.*

Human beings are in constant contact with other beings: some are perceptible, while others cannot be perceived by our senses.

Beings that are perceptible and palpable to us are the animals, plants, and minerals. In the levels of the process of spiritual perfection, these beings are less evolved than humans, and each species communicates among itself through its own particular language. Those who are sufficiently awake spiritually can find that these beings are endowed with their own feelings and specific senses, even those that are apparently inanimate (such as minerals). For example, animals are endowed with precise senses with which they can predict certain natural disasters or aggressions such as war; some domestic animals such as dogs can sense the death of their owners ahead of time.

Each of these beings, within its own limits, is endowed with an innate aptitude to comprehend the presence of the Creator and to establish contact with Him. Even minerals—which are supposedly inanimate—sense His presence and have feelings of joy or unhappiness, each in its own special way. For example, the grounds on which a house of worship is constructed, or land on which food is cultivated, has a joyous state, for it feels that it is being used for a beneficial purpose.

In general, the various beings on earth, with the exception of humans, live in a constant state of joy and happiness.

Rational Beings

Human beings are not the only rational beings in the material universe: there are innumerable planets populated by rational inhabitants. These beings more or less resemble humans, and some of them are familiar with the planet earth.

In addition to humans, there also exist other rational beings on earth. Created prior to us, these intelligent beings have a different constitution than ours and are imperceptible by our ordinary senses.[1]

Among these beings, there are groups that inherently feel enmity toward humans. Their coexistence with humans is somewhat similar to that of microorganisms with us: although they are constantly in contact with us, as long as we are healthy and our immune system is strong they do not cause us any harm. As soon as our immune system weakens, however, these microorganisms attack and cause various illnesses. Similarly, as long as our self or psychospiritual organism is healthy and our spiritual immune system is working well, these beings remain harmless. Once antispiritual thoughts weaken our faith in the Source, however, we become susceptible to their attacks. Anyone who is influenced by such beings will be subject to various spiritual, psychological, familial, and social difficulties.

There also exist other invisible beings that do not live on earth, but they, too, can establish contact with us. Angels, for example, have corporeal images through which they can sometimes manifest themselves to us, like the two angels that appeared to Abraham and Lot. According to sacred traditions, before the creation of humans, angels were the highest beings, and their rank is still higher than that of humans. Through their own wrongdoing, human beings can fall to a level below the basest of creatures; once they reach perfection, however, they attain a higher level than angels, for to reach perfection they must traverse a longer path and overcome more difficult obstacles.

Beings commonly known as "guardian angels" are those that have the temperament of angels and the mission of watching over and helping human beings. In some cultures, each child has a guardian angel to protect him during his childhood, but at the end of this period the angel's help becomes contingent upon the behavior of the adolescent. The "angel of the home" that protects sincere and united families belongs to this group of angels.[2]

THE PATH OF PERFECTION

- ❖ Spiritual Pitfalls

- ❖ Guidance

- ❖ Spiritual Techniques

- ❖ Fighting Against the Imperious Self

- ❖ Self-Knowledge

- ❖ The Spiritual Student

- ❖ The Path of Perfection at a Glance

34. SPIRITUAL PITFALLS

> *Do not imagine that sabotage exists only in the material world; we should be even more wary of those spiritual criminals.*

In our day and age, numerous paths are offered toward spirituality. Since most people do not have a correct gauge in hand, it is difficult, indeed sometimes impossible, to distinguish the right path from the wrong ones. For those in search of spirituality, therefore, there is a high likelihood of being misled and getting entangled in fatal paths. Those who fall into the traps of spiritual opportunists or become toys in the hands of "tempter spirits" usually consider their imperious desires as "legitimate spiritual wishes."

Tempter Spirits

In every method (meditation, asceticism, psychological experiences, etc.) used to acquire the quality of self-consciousness—or even when such a state automatically appears as a result of simply establishing contact with the world of spirits—tempter spirits are the first to approach us. Assigned with the mission of testing those who step foot into the world of spirits, tempter spirits target an individual's weak points, preoccupy him with chimerical thoughts, and strengthen his pride through a variety of means. For example, they may suggest to an individual that he is one of the elite, or that he has a spiritual mission and is endowed with powers and miracles.[1] These souls enchant human beings, but have nothing to offer them except nonsense. By subjugating the souls of vulnerable individuals, they can manifest themselves directly or suggest whatever they desire through inspirations, intuitions, voices, etc.;[2] they can also affect us indirectly through a deluded master, a false guide, and the like.

There is nothing more attractive and pleasing for the imperious self than to believe the enticements of the tempter spirits, for they are well-informed about an individual's weak points and know how to manipulate them. Someone who falls into the trap of these spirits is seduced and a state similar to an addiction arises within him; spiritually, the individual is considered lost, at least in this lifetime.

Every human being encounters tempter spirits along the path toward perfection. Those who are alert pass this test successfully and safely enter the next stage, especially if a true guide is preserving and protecting them. Those who lack such protection, however, should take the following points into account:

♦ To want the Source for the sake of the Source, meaning our goal and desire should be divine satisfaction.

♦ To be prudent and judicious in choosing a spiritual path.

♦ To avoid any guide or master who uses spirituality as a means of deriving income and securing his livelihood. There are also other tangible signs a seeker should pay attention to: Does the guide practice what he preaches? Is he hungry for money and power? Does he have a weakness for luxury? Is he selfish and enslaved by his imperious self? Is he lascivious? Is he a megalomaniac?

♦ To consider spirituality as the science of the process of spiritual perfection, not as a tool for entertainment or experiencing ecstatic states and visions, acquiring altered states of consciousness, or performing miracles, wonders, stupendous acts, etc.

Deluded Guides

Deluded guides refers to those individuals who unconsciously become entangled in the trap of the temptations of negative spirits, especially tempter spirits, due to their naiveté and thirst for power. Although such individuals may have some spiritual powers (wonders) at the outset, they rapidly expend them to keep their disciples satisfied. After squandering their spiritual reserves, they resort to various techniques to maintain control over their disciples. If there is any truth in the teachings of such guides in the beginning, they quickly become devoid of truth and are led astray.

False Guides

If deluded guides are sincere to the extent that they believe in their own mission, at least at the outset, the same cannot be said for false guides, who are devious opportunists. Based on the ever increasing need of human beings for spirituality, they use the credulity or naiveté of individuals as a tool for deceiving them by posing as spiritual guides in order to secure their own personal interests. False guides imitate the external behavior of saints of the past. Devoid of any spirituality, they possess only some unusual powers acquired through parapsychology or paraspiritual techniques such as hypnotism, magnetism, meditation, etc.; most of them use psychotropic substances as well.

False guides do not lead anyone to the Source.[3] Someone who steps onto a false spiritual path, even if with sincerity, is searching for a treasure in a place where it doesn't exist. Although he takes on many hardships, ultimately he gets nowhere. For a human being to advance spiritually, it is not sufficient to merely have faith in a path and to act upon that faith; rather, that path must culminate in a truth. To reach the truth, one must have faith in a real truth, not an imaginary one, and must put that real truth into practice.

Most people who are deceived by false paths and guides have committed wrongs themselves, whether in this life or past lives.

For example, someone who causes others to lose their faith will become a follower of false guides, false paths, or false religions in subsequent lives.

The Source exposes the trickery of deceptive spiritual leaders—this is a divine law. Nevertheless, few are willing to accept this and to adopt prudence and a sound mind as their gauge, to open their eyes, and to see the imposter.

Esoteric "Experts"

Esoteric "experts" refers to those seekers who consider theoretical knowledge to be sufficient for knowing mysticism. Although such scholars generally have vast theoretical knowledge, mystical knowledge is achieved only through spiritual understanding, which cannot be realized without practice and experience.

In this realm, relying solely on theory is similar to wanting to become a master musician solely by learning the scales, or speaking a foreign language merely by memorizing the dictionary. Consequently, although the knowledge of such "experts" may contain some theoretical truths, it is devoid of any kind of spiritual cohesiveness and thus lacks practical value.

Wanderers

Some individuals do not want to commit themselves to a place, path, or method and are under the impression they can personally create their own specific path. This mindset draws them to different schools, and they take away something from each one. Such "patchwork spirituality" does not reflect the real truth. Moreover, other than a few exceptional cases affirmed by the Source, no human being alone is capable of confronting the tests and traps that are an inherent part of the spiritual path. As a result of not having a protective guide, such individuals are subject to spiritual bewilderment and chronic confusion without realizing it, and may even lose the faith they initially had. Many also reach a point where they mistakenly consider themselves to be guides.

Spiritual traps and negative spirits lie in wait to prey on spiritual seekers.[4] Faced with these dangers, the only effective safeguard is the supervision and protection of a true guide. True guides exist all over the world, but it is difficult to find them as they normally avoid commotion and fame and do not want to attract people's attention or that of the media. If someone does not have access to a true guide, the wisest approach is to act upon the principles of his own faith and to focus his attention on the unique Source. If he does not adhere to a particular faith, it is better to observe ethical principles and to live according to his conscience, for not believing in the Source or a spiritual path is less harmful than believing in a false path or practicing a deviated mysticism. The goal of mysticism is self-knowledge—that is, to understand who we are, where we have come from, what our duties are in this world, and where we are going. Once an individual comes to know himself, he will also know the Source and will enter the stages of the path of perfection, where he will persevere until he reaches perfection.

35. GUIDANCE

> *A true spiritual guide is like a physician who gives each person the medicine that corresponds to his condition and capacity.*

Those who are determined to advance in spirituality must first know what spirituality is. Spirituality is the science of the process of spiritual perfection—the science of preserving the health and natural growth of the celestial soul. Unfortunately, whenever there is a discussion of spirituality, notions that have more of a theatrical aspect, ecstatic states, divination, and the like immediately come to mind;[1] some individuals also seek psychological tranquility in spirituality. Rare, however, are those who recognize spirituality as a scientific method for the preservation of the soul's development and health—that is, as the *medicine of the soul*, whose goal is the process of perfection of the celestial soul and the return of human beings to their Source. To reach this goal, one must believe in the truth and seek to absorb and assimilate the authentic divine and ethical principles that have been taught by the divine envoys. It is at that point that we begin to realize the obstacles that await us on the path, and the impossibility of passing through them without the grace of guidance; hence, the tremendous importance of correctly choosing our "guidance."

Guidance

The Source is the educator of all worlds. In order for human beings to receive the teachings that would enable them to reach spiritual perfection, the Source makes His guidance available on earth at all times. There is no mission more vital and sensitive than spiritual guidance, which requires that the guide himself know the Source. On earth, this guidance has been entrusted to his representative or *Vali*: one whose words and decisions are the words and decisions of the Source.[2] According to the principle of causality, divine light (**metacausal energy** and guidance) is reflected through the Vali of the time and spread to all of the beings on earth. The rest of the authentic spiritual guides, teachers, and instructors who can be found across the world as needed receive their metacausal energy through the Vali, even if they are unaware of the relationship connecting them to him. Just as people benefit from electrical energy without knowing its origin, these spiritual guides also receive metacausal energy from the Vali, even if they do not know its exact source. At times, some of them become aware of the existence of a spiritual entity giving them such energy, but since they do not know of the Vali, they imagine this entity to be one of the saints or envoys from their own religion, whereas in reality it is the light of the Vali they see in this manner, the same individual who holds the cord of divine guidance on earth.

Such guidance is specific to human beings. Considering that our thought evolves over time, the external appearance of divine guidance—and not the truth of its core,[3] which always remains constant—must also evolve to remain compatible with the thought of those to whom it is addressed. In our era, guidance should be based on "rationality" and presented in a university format.[4] To be guided today, an individual must use his mind and free will rather than accepting matters out of blind obedience in a dogmatic fashion devoid of comprehension. In our times, spiritual teachings should respect an individual's freedom of thought, be comprehensible and rational, and help each person to develop his own faculty of spiritual discernment.

Consequently, we should expect from this point forward that spiritual teachings will increasingly take shape through scientific exchanges within a university format. The legitimacy of the ancient master-disciple system is constantly decreasing and will gradually be replaced by the university-student system. Once this system falls into place, it will become possible to realistically assess each person's spiritual level, just as it is possible to assess the scientific level of students or teachers today in any branch of science. Nonetheless, the origin of guidance (divine light) is always the Vali: it is he who is, and will always be, the guardian of divine teachings on earth, whether the people of his time recognize him or not.

The Benefit of a Guide

The psychospiritual organism of human beings, similar to their biological organism, can also suffer functional impairments and various illnesses. For example, pride and doubt are among the most difficult illnesses of the psychospiritual organism to cure. If these two illnesses take root in the soul, any spiritual measure to treat them will result in failure, for progress in spirituality requires humility and resolve. Illnesses of the celestial soul manifest at the level of the mind through different signs: a weakening of faith to the point of atheism, reduced willpower, decreased spiritual motivation, etc. According to the law of connected vessels, the weakening of the celestial soul automatically strengthens and excites the imperious self, which then takes control of the reins of reason and willpower.

Authentic spirituality is like the medicine of the soul. Whenever our body becomes ill, we consult with a physician; likewise, if our celestial soul becomes ill, we should also consult with a physician of the soul. Only a true spiritual physician can properly cure an individual's soul, for he knows the specific remedy for treating each illness. If we do not have access to such a physician, we can resort to the Divinity of the Time, who is always present. To do so, it is not necessary to personally know him; each person can find Him within himself. The Divinity of the Time often cures individuals without they themselves realizing it, and they only feel its beneficial effects.

In order for a prescribed treatment to result in the health of the celestial soul, it must contain the *divine impact,* which is concealed in *divine authorization.* Such authorization is given by the Divinity of the Time to his Vali, who in turn can place it at the disposal of guides, instructors, and anyone else he may deem fit. The active ingredient in these spiritual medicines (prescriptions) is the divine impact. In addition, the divine impact prevents an ill person from being harmed by the potential errors of an authorized guide.[5]

Benefiting from divine guidance is similar to the state of a person who, having been lost in a dense fog with no visibility, suddenly sees a light that points him in the right direction. He shouldn't turn away from this light, but instead should carefully listen to the instructions of the guide so he can pass through the obstacles and traps that lie ahead of him on the path.

It should be noted that the Divinity of the Time transcends the Vali and the guides.[6] He is the source of light for the Vali and all of the guides, closely supervising the state of all seekers of truth, regardless of their faith and convictions. If someone invokes Him, he will receive an answer and assistance, and his pain will be cured. Based on the law of causality, the Divinity of the Time guides his beings however He deems best, whether through the Vali or His other emissaries, or through other means appropriate to each person's state.

The Characteristics of Authentic Guides

In our day and age, authentic guides are quite rare and recognizing them is particularly difficult, for they prefer to avoid fame and live away from the spotlight of the media. To find divine guidance, the best means is to plead to the Divinity of the Time or, if someone believes in a particular faith, to seek help from its envoy or one of its saints. If someone is devoted to the Source and sincerely asks for His guidance, the Divinity of the Time will help him discern the authenticity of the guidance, whether through inspiration, intuition, enlightenment, or any other means deemed appropriate.

Certain criteria also exist for discerning the authenticity of true guides. These criteria are applicable provided we try to set aside our preconceptions and observe things carefully. An authentic guide must have control over his nature (id), and his words should bear the divine impact. Having the divine impact is itself a sign of divine approval. In addition, a true guide should also "fear the Source" and act upon what he recommends to others.[7] He should not be egotistical, but upright, sincere, just, and humble, and should earn his livelihood through his own work. Although he can be financially secure, under no circumstances should he ever use spirituality as a means of earning money for himself, and he should always act upon the essence of the teachings relayed by the divine envoys.

36. SPIRITUAL TECHNIQUES

Suppressing or weakening the terrestrial soul is no extraordinary feat; what counts is to have such control over it through the force of our will-power that we no longer innately desire that which is beneath the dignity of our soul.

A uthentic spirituality is neither a means for seeking power nor a tool for discoveries and wonders or mystifying performances. It is also not a means for achieving ecstasy or a tool for recreation or entering trance-like states, much less a tranquilizer for alleviating disturbed psyches. Nor for that matter is spirituality a theatrical art, unusual acts, or parapsychology. In reality, authentic spirituality is the science of life that teaches us how to preserve the health of our psychospiritual organism and to secure the natural development of our celestial soul through an active and beneficial social life in order to advance toward our perfection. Instead of thinking about spirituality as a science for the health and development of the celestial soul, however, the image people have of spirituality nowadays is more about discoveries and wonders, mystifying displays of power, or ecstatic or peaceful states achieved through various meditative techniques, despite the fact that such states not only fail to develop the celestial soul but actually harm its natural growth.

The Trap of Spiritual Techniques
Spiritual techniques—whether meditative in nature, used in conjunction with asceticism, or accompanied by psychotropic substances—are always intended to produce an altered state of

consciousness. Such techniques have always been accessible to everyone and remain so today. With the help of these techniques and substances, anyone can open a window to the other world and acquire certain intuitive states or establish contact with spirits. In some of the techniques for acquiring unusual powers, energy is also derived from one's own physical-psychological energy, but there is no trace of spirituality in any of them. Still other techniques originate from the superficial imitation of the perceived actions of some great saints and mystics of the past. For example, some believe that by imitating mystics—those so overwhelmed at the level of connecting with the Source that they either lost all movement and remained silent or were led to dance—they too will benefit from the same spiritual result.

In all these cases, the main outcome of such methods is solely the creation of altered states of consciousness. Although the psychological effects of these techniques at times appear to be significant (a reduction in stress, for example), we should realize their results are fleeting. While the stress and anxiety of an individual is temporarily alleviated, once the technique is discontinued, they will return sooner or later with an even greater impact.

In addition, the effect of spiritual techniques on the celestial soul in general is similar to the influence of drugs and tranquilizers on the body and psyche. By producing ephemeral states of attraction, ecstasy, imagination, exhilaration, and serenity, these techniques artificially quench the celestial soul's thirst for understanding the truth. In reality, the growth of the soul, like that of the body, must take place naturally; spiritual and paranormal techniques, however, have no place in the natural development of the soul and even create a state of addiction that weakens and ultimately halts its growth. Furthermore, prior to reaching a sufficient level of spiritual maturity, supernatural powers or visions resulting from such techniques are harmful for an individual and immerse him in self-satisfaction, self-centeredness, and other such qualities.

Ultimately, having visions and contacting spirits without knowing whom or what one is dealing with, and entering the unknown realm of spirits without knowing where one is going, subject an individual to grave spiritual dangers. One of these dangers is the existence of tempter spirits and hostile spirits that naturally surround anyone who enters the invisible world. These spirits encompass an individual and can control his mind, relaying to him anything they wish.

Asceticism and Mortification

In the past, the prevalent methods of the mystics were mostly based on withdrawing from the world, secluding oneself from society, and engaging in asceticism and mortification. Similarly, in our day and age there are numerous individuals who adhere to more or less the same form of classical mysticism. If the body is weakened through ascetic practices, the dominance of the impulses and desires of the self (the id or terrestrial soul) will inevitably be weakened and the intervening veil between the psyche and the celestial soul will become less opaque. In such a state, an ascetic feels a pseudo-mystical happiness and can even establish contact with the world of spirits. But how does such a state help the growth of the celestial soul? This method of repressing the desires of the self through physical ascetic practices results in the abnormal growth of only a part of the self, while the other parts remain underdeveloped and thus create an imbalance in the self as a whole.

The best method for developing the celestial soul is to maintain a balance between the desires of the celestial soul, on the one hand, and the legitimate desires of the terrestrial soul (body), on the other.[1] Consider the celestial soul as a rider who has to undertake an extremely long and perilous journey, and whose only "mount" is the terrestrial soul. If the balance noted above is established and the terrestrial soul is strong but obedient, meaning the mount is powerful yet tame, the rider can guide it and travel in the right direction, in which case he will rapidly proceed toward his destination and will have benefited from all of the opportunities for progress. If the celestial soul submits to the terrestrial soul, however, the mount will become powerful but unruly and control will fall into the hands of the imperious self, which will then lead the celestial soul wherever it wants. Through privation and mortification, the ascetic places his body into a deplorable state: the mount is so weak it no longer has the strength to even rise, yet it is not under the command of the rider, either. As soon as the ascetic stops his practices, the terrestrial soul remobilizes, becomes stronger, and its impulses and desires become more active than before.[2]

From a different perspective, the celestial soul, like a fetus that grows in its mother's womb, must undergo its stages of development in the biological body (terrestrial womb). The effect of spiritual techniques such as asceticism and meditation on the soul is like that of hormones on the growth of the fetus, an excessive amount of which can have dire consequences. Therefore, if we want the development of our soul to follow its natural process, we should avoid stringent ascetic practices as well as any kind of spiritual techniques or drugs. The best method for the harmonious growth of the self is "natural spirituality."

Education of Thought

With the help of their willpower, today's human beings are capable of overcoming the impulses of their imperious self, provided that such willpower derives from their celestial reason.[3] In natural spirituality, physical asceticism has no application, and is replaced by a task called *education of thought*. Despite living an active life in society and constantly being subject to various temptations, a correct education of thought enables an individual to gradually overcome the impulses of the imperious self through the use of his willpower and help from the Source, thereby ensuring the *natural* growth of the celestial soul. In addition to nourishing the celestial soul, carefully practicing authentic divine principles and ethics provides the energy necessary for strengthening one's willpower.

Natural Spiritual States

It is possible for an individual to automatically experience certain spiritual states without desiring them or using any specific techniques. It sometimes happens that without any preparation or will, a person experiences a state of joyous bliss that brings illumination and heartfelt warmth, a feeling that may soon disappear. He may also receive inspirations, ones so subtle that at first he may confuse them with his own self-suggestions or consider them to be a figment of his imagination. It is possible, however, to identify an inspiration with the help of certain specific signs: inspirations come to mind suddenly and without any previous preparation; they influence one's mind such that it is not possible to alter them or willfully remove them from one's thoughts; and they contain truths that can often be verified.

At higher levels, one may sense a fragrance, feel the blowing of a breeze, hear a sound or words, and even experience visions—states many mystics have actually experienced.[4] If one does not pay more attention than necessary to such experiences and pursues education of thought with seriousness and persistence like a diligent student, he will develop the aptitude to interpret such phenomena.

These states and experiences rarely occur, and their presence or absence is not contingent upon the degree of the celestial soul's development: a person can develop his celestial soul without experiencing such states. It is possible for certain individuals to be quite advanced spiritually, but to have neither visions nor inspirations. In reality, experiencing such states depends on an individual's psychospiritual constitution and the divine will.

On the other hand, when someone entrusts the spiritual guidance of his celestial soul to the Source, he will usually be prevented from having such contacts with the other world, for the self-satisfaction and egotism that would ensue would hamper his progress. In any case, it is not right to induce such states through specific techniques or methods, for the danger of being led astray by them is extremely high.

In summary, what human beings should seek in spirituality is light, not power. Divine light nourishes the celestial soul and results in its growth and proximity to the Source, while seeking spiritual power nourishes the terrestrial soul and prevents the growth of the celestial soul, distancing one from the Source: with the former (light), human beings become humble and softhearted; with the latter (power), they become self-centered and megalomaniacal.

37. Fighting Against the Imperious Self

> *The path of perfection can be summarized in two points: constant attention to the Source and fighting against the imperious self.*

If we are to advance spiritually, we must clearly combine theory with practice, for practice alone is insufficient and theory by itself accomplishes little. Practicing spirituality, in essence, is none other than fighting against the imperious self,[1] which arises from the terrestrial soul or id situated in the realm of the unconscious.[2] The imperious self is the source of harmful, anti-ethical, and anti-divine impulses. While the approach of classical mysticism entailed drying up this source by repressing and weakening the body and subjecting oneself to physical and psychological deprivation, the method of natural spirituality is exactly the opposite: instead of repressing and weakening the body, we strengthen it, and with the willpower of a stronger soul guided by celestial reason, we seek to dominate the illegitimate desires of the imperious self. It is through this natural process that we can transform the character units of our psychospiritual organism or self into divine virtues and evolve our transcendent reason into celestial reason.[3]

The Imperious Self
As long as the celestial soul has not reached a certain degree of maturity, we cannot discover the existence of the imperious self within ourselves. At the conscious level, the imperious self manifests as successive impulses of illegitimate and harmful desires of the

terrestrial soul (id), imposing its capricious whims—which it seeks to immediately gratify—with full force while constantly fighting against and opposing the guidance of our celestial reason.

One of the characteristics of the imperious self is its use of various tactics to dominate the ego or celestial soul. The imperious self usually derives all the power for its attacks through its animal desires and whims, but sometimes it deceitfully takes on the garment of reason and speaks through that voice as well. If someone is unaware of this, he will deceive himself in such cases by justifying his whims through logical reasoning or some other disingenuous rationalization. This is the highest level of deviation, for the individual assists his imperious self by creating his own justifications to make his whimsical desires appear legitimate, and then devises disingenuous reasons to surrender to those desires. For example, someone who intentionally avoids declaring part of his income on his tax return justifies his action on the basis that he is already paying a substantial amount in taxes. Or when someone takes something from a wealthy person, his imperious self immediately declares there is nothing wrong with such an action, for he is doing so in a state of need and distress. In this manner, the imperious self makes stealing appear permissible. Someone who procrastinates in repaying a debt justifies his action on the basis that his intention is not to avoid repaying the debt.

Another trick the imperious self employs is to appear as if it has retreated, thus deceiving the individual into thinking it has surrendered. But this retreat is merely a ploy, a ruse through which it seeks to undo the person's defenses and make him negligent so it can later attack the individual when his guard is down.

The imperious self's methods for dominating men and women differ. Among women, the imperious self mostly works through emotions, especially through their impressionability, jealousy, and vengefulness. Among men, however, the imperious self attacks above all through pride, the quest for power, and lasciviousness.

These weak points can cause an uninformed individual to lose in an instant everything he has worked hard to spiritually gain over the years. The history of religions is replete with such moments of weakness (infamous temptations).

In addition to some of the psychological weaknesses noted above, other weaknesses such as a love of money, seeking honors, ostentation, etc., make an individual more vulnerable to the imperious self. For those who have reached a certain level in the spiritual world, fighting against the imperious self is even more complex, for spiritual self-satisfaction and megalomania are added to these weaknesses and can lead a person to become entirely dominated by his imperious self.

It is in the daily tests of life that fighting against the imperious self takes on meaning. These tests, which are regulated by the divine causal system, are of different natures, but in all cases they aim at an individual's weak points. As such, most of the events that occur in daily life, even small incidents, are in reality scenes for testing and purifying an individual so he can discover a new corner of his being each time and come to better know himself. These tests may be internal (e.g., a negative intention that he must combat) or they may manifest as dreams (e.g., a person dreams he is encountered with a temptation and his reaction to this temptation is thus examined).

The Benefit of the Imperious Self

Although the imperious self is considered as the main enemy of the celestial soul, its existence is necessary for the growth of the soul, for without opposition and struggle, the growth of the celestial soul or ego cannot take place. The desires of the imperious self are analogous to bacterial toxins: if the toxins are strong and in large quantities, they will be harmful and perhaps even fatal for the celestial soul, but if they are weakened and in small doses they help vaccinate the soul against the imperious self and enable it to gradually control the impulses of the imperious self.

How to Fight Against the Imperious Self

A natural tendency exists within the celestial soul to draw closer to the divine Source, just as there is a natural tendency in the imperious self to distance itself from the Source. While the celestial soul must make a willful and constant effort through the conscious ego to carry out its objectives, the imperious self, which originates from the id and is situated in the realm of the unconscious, does not need to exert any effort, for its actions are instinctual and automatic. Faced with the attacks of the imperious self, the main work of the conscious ego is to remain alert and not to allow the imperious self to impose its rule by overtaking one's reason and willpower. If someone disregards his imperious self due to ignorance, negligence, or indifference and remains passive, the struggle between his celestial and terrestrial parts will unconsciously shift toward control by the imperious self, to the extent that the imperious self will completely dominate his celestial soul. What is even more dangerous is that most people are unaware of this domination of the imperious self over them.

Successfully fighting against the imperious self requires a correct approach. On one hand, a human being must analyze his psyche to become aware of his faults and weaknesses and the presence of the imperious self; on the other hand, he must preserve the health of his ego and develop it until he acquires a strong willpower and a sound mind.[4]

In practice, we must first fight against the character flaws or psychospiritual weak points that are more prominent. As a result of fighting against each of these weak points, other weak points will manifest themselves. Thus, in this manner we can gradually come to know the various facets of the imperious self and neutralize its attacks and tricks. Among the various methods of fighting against the imperious self, one is to systematically oppose its desires at the outset and to perform their exact opposite. For example, if someone dislikes another person, each time he is tempted to speak ill of him he should initially force himself to resist, and at a higher level he should only mention the person's positive points. If he perseveres in doing so, his negative feelings about him will gradually disappear.

Fighting against the imperious self (character flaws or psychospiritual weak points) is a long process and requires a great deal of persistence. To maintain the necessary motivation, socializing with spiritually positive people, helping others, acts of charity, studying divine texts, pilgrimages, and prayer are all beneficial factors in strengthening our resolve.

The main weapons of the ego against the imperious self are a resolute will, divine ethics, and divine principles. The application of divine ethics and divine principles provides the necessary nutrients for the growth of our psychospiritual organism. Only in the heat of this internal struggle do we realize that without divine help, we cannot obtain any permanent, tangible result, and that without divine protection and light, our willpower alone is incapable of accomplishing anything. It is by having faith in the true Source that we can absorb His light, which contains guidance and energy; without such light, the continuous suppression of the impulses of the imperious self will result in repulsion and the creation of complexes and other psychological problems. The divine regard neutralizes the harmful psychological effects that result from such suppression.

38. SELF-KNOWLEDGE

Delve within until you find the Source, for to know the Source one must first know oneself.

Before discussing self-knowledge, it is necessary to briefly explain divine knowledge.

Divine Knowledge

The specific sense within human beings that recognizes truth and understands the essential reality of each thing beyond its appearance is an acquired one—that is, each person must actualize this potential himself. Resulting from the maturation of the celestial soul, this distinct sense includes different degrees, ranging from a simple feeling to perceiving the exact truth to ultimately joining the Truth.[1] Someone who is even at the preliminary stages of awakening this sense will not be deceived by false or deviated spiritual paths and masters, for he has experienced the fragrance of knowing the truth. Nor will the false principles attributed to the Source appeal to him, even if mixed with the teachings of divine religions. Subsequently, at the level of exact observation, he will see and recognize the Source within himself: that is when he has reached divine knowledge.

Divine knowledge is not possible solely through the ordinary (terrestrial) intellect and the acquisition of theoretical knowledge; rather, such knowledge constitutes a higher level. An individual may be familiar with all the theories and have mastered them as well, yet still remain at the beginner levels in the science of divine knowledge, like the great scientists who have not developed the sense of knowing the Source within themselves and therefore deny any kind of divine quality or even become followers of a false spiritual path.

Divine knowledge, then, is a specific sense that is obtained only through acting upon *divine spirituality,* and it is through the process of delving within and knowing oneself that this sense is cultivated.[2]

Self-Knowledge

The path culminating in divine knowledge necessarily passes through the realm of self-knowledge. In other words, to develop the specific sense of knowing the Source, one must first delve within until he comes to know his own self. As an individual gradually advances in his self-knowledge, the first rays of divine knowledge (the level of sensation) reach his conscious mind.

To know the self, we first have to know what it is and from which source it originates. The self is a psychospiritual organism that comes into existence from the fusion of the terrestrial and celestial souls. A living, dynamic, and evolving entity, the psychospiritual organism is comprised of several components[3] originating from the celestial soul—namely, the ego, the superego, and the super id—and a single component originating from the terrestrial soul, the id [Figure 2, p. 36].[4]

◆ The ego, which constitutes a major component of the celestial soul, is the origin of reason, realism, and the conscious mind, and is almost synonymous with the self. The ego of our present life gradually takes form during childhood by encountering the realities of life. Our present ego is under the influence of the egos of our past lives, which have been preserved in the unconscious and transferred through the "genetic inheritance" of our celestial soul.[5] Subject to the principle of realism, the ego can refuse the impulses of the id (terrestrial soul) or delay their gratification. The ego is the potential ruler of our being: if it shows weakness and cannot control the id, however, the id will take its place and govern us instead.

♦ The id is a psychological and instinctual component that is the origin of terrestrial energy, vital instincts, and animal impulses in human beings.[6] Subject to the pleasure principle, it abhors discomfort, suffering, and deprivation, insisting instead upon the immediate and complete satisfaction of its needs, impulses, and desires. If the desires of the id are not controlled by the ego, the celestial soul will gradually become poisoned and may even reach the threshold of ruin. In contrast to the ego, which is formed in a gradual manner by encountering realities, the id manifests at once and in an innate way, accompanying a human being from the very outset. The id manifests in the conscious with two facets: the first is the imperious self, the source of animal impulses and whimsical desires that are harmful for the celestial soul and considered to be the main enemy of our ego on the spiritual path;[7] the second is the worker self, which is the origin of our vital needs and responsible for our biological survival.[8]

♦ The superego, a component of the celestial soul that is part instinctual and part educable, is formed of three consciences: the blaming conscience, the inspiring conscience, and the certifying conscience. The correct functioning of the blaming conscience (the voice of our conscience) depends a great deal on the education it is given throughout its present life, as well as the genetic aptitude of the celestial soul that it carries from its past lives. That is why some children are endowed with a strong voice of conscience while others are practically devoid of one and do not feel any regret for their improper actions. The superego is a necessary friend and helper of the ego, which needs this energy in order to control the free rein and constant desires of the imperious self.

♦ The super id is also a component of the celestial soul and serves as the source of its impulses. The tendencies of the super id are in direct opposition to those of the id.[9] Like the id, the super id is governed by the pleasure principle, only in this case supernatural (spiritual) pleasures. If the super id remains healthy and is properly governed by the ego, it will manifest itself in the conscious as faith and love of the Source, altruism, etc., and will serve as a source of positive energy of a celestial nature that is necessary for fighting the imperious self. If the super id is not controlled by the ego, however, it will lead toward excess (mystical excess).[10] When an individual becomes entangled in deviated spiritualities, the super id is overtaken by the imperious self: in such a state, its supernatural tendencies will be drawn in the direction induced by the imperious self. For example, the hubbub and psychospiritual displays of power of deviated and false spiritual schools become attractive and mesmerize him, whereas the desire for true spirituality becomes extremely weak within him.

Once a human being distinguishes the different structural components of his being and each of their tendencies, he must familiarize himself with the manifestations of each of these components, particularly the excesses and deficiencies of the id (especially the imperious self). In other words, through careful and profound observation and analysis of one's inner self, each person must find his own positive and negative potentials with regard to ethics and spirituality, and accurately assess his own attributes, positive qualities, strong points, flaws, weak points, etc.

Flaws and weak points are like dark stains that cause imbalances within us and alter the transparency of the psychospiritual organism or self. These stains blur and obscure a person's inner being and prevent him from knowing his self. As an individual gradually discovers the factors behind this imbalance (obscurity), he has to seek to eliminate them. To do so, the ego must above all identify one by one the functioning of the psychospiritual components of the self and distinguish the needs of each, fulfilling legitimate needs and controlling illegitimate ones. To accomplish this task, the ego needs reference points and role models. The reference points are the correct ethical principles and authentic divine teachings that show us the excess and deficiency of each matter, while the reliable role models are the great divine saints, whether from the past or the present, who embody these principles. In our time, gaining access to such individuals is not an easy task, but someone who is sincere and pure with the Source will either find them or be led to understand in a manner He deems best.

At this point the ego, which has become activated by the positive energy of the super id, must work hard to control the animal impulses and desires of the id with the help of reason and the self's transcendent willpower, as well as the assistance of the superego, without neglecting the constant danger of the mystical excesses of the super id.[11] It should also be emphasized that the ego alone is incapable of imposing its will for an extended period of time upon the uncontrolled impulses and desires of the id, particularly the imperious self, unless it receives direct help from the Source. Without such help, the ego can never achieve a permanent spiritual result. The impulses of the imperious self that arise from the id are in reality subject to causal processes, the permanent control of which is contingent upon receiving the metacausal energy of divine help.[12]

In summary, to reach divine knowledge, one must first acquire self-knowledge. To know oneself, at the outset one must pay attention to and identify the different components that form the self and learn how each manifests in the realm of the conscious. As an individual gradually becomes aware of the imbalances in his attributes, he has to decrease them through the imposition of his willpower. To succeed in this task and achieve a definitive result requires reliable reference points and role models, and in particular direct divine assistance (metacausal energy).

Each time an individual overcomes one of his weak points or flaws, it transforms into a luminous point in the realm of the unconscious, as though a small candle has been lit there. However small this candle may be, its light will spread throughout the unconscious, and the individual can thus perceive his inner self a little more clearly. Whenever these points of light reach a sufficient number, the unconscious will become illuminated, enabling one to see within and to better know oneself.

Accordingly, throughout the process of self-knowledge we gradually become familiar with our celestial soul and realize it is that which gives *me* life; that which constitutes *my* ego; that which causes *me* to think, reason, comprehend, and exist; that which is eternal and remains eternal, for it is endowed with a particle that comes from the source of life. This source that I now behold once more is due to the existence of my certifying conscience, which gives me certitude about the truth of this source. It is from this point on that I understand who I am, where I have come from, what my duties are, and where I am going.

As the ego gradually succeeds in controlling the various impulses of the imperious self due to the growth of celestial reason and an increase in willpower, the unconscious becomes more translucent and we come to better know ourselves. In this state, the dark realm of our unconscious becomes smaller and smaller, and the extent of our total consciousness expands. From then on, the celestial soul's specific yet potential sense of seeing the truth—the only means through which we can know the Source—is realized and activated, and higher levels of divine knowledge are achieved until the individual acquires complete certainty. If we continue progressing in this task of self-knowledge, the celestial soul's other senses will gradually be awakened as well and the veil separating them from the physical senses will be removed; we can then reach the level of exact observation, for the Source can only be seen and recognized with the eyes of the soul, not those of the body. Thus, it is by reaching complete self-knowledge that we can see and recognize Him.

In conclusion, we can use another example in which the self or psychospiritual organism is analogized to a volume of limpid water that we wish to sweeten to the point of saturation. Each time we assimilate an ethical principle within the self, it is as if we have added some sugar to the water; naturally, the sugar will permeate the entire volume of water and sweeten it. Accordingly, each time we assimilate an ethical or divine principle, it permeates the entire self and makes us more aware of ourselves and the Source. In addition to adding sugar, we also have to heat the solution to complete the saturation process. Similarly, to complete the process of assimilating ethical and divine principles to the point where we reach divine knowledge, we have to warm the self with the light of the Source. Without this light, self-knowledge will not be possible, and without self-knowledge we will not reach the state of self-consciousness necessary for divine knowledge. The way to receive divine light is to turn our attention toward the Source.

The ultimate level of knowledge, then, is when the solution of our being has become saturated with ethical and divine principles and each of them has been assimilated within the self one by one. It is in this state that we reach divine knowledge and, saturated by the bliss of such knowledge, want nothing more than what we are.

39. The Spiritual Student

A spiritual student is one who is thirsty for the Truth.

Each person goes to the other world just as he is here and with the same perception. If we do not comprehend spiritual truths in this world, we will not do so in the other world either, and we will find ourselves in a state of sorrow, wandering and lost. In reality, knowledge of a purely physical or material nature has no application in the spiritual world; pseudodivine knowledge is similarly devoid of any value, merely adding to one's confusion, while anti-divine knowledge serves as a heavy load that reduces the vastness of our field of perception, intensifies our confusion, and creates additional sorrow and suffering.[1] In general, each person is confined to his own field of perception in the spiritual world.

Of the knowledge acquired during earthly life, only the recognition of divine truths expands an individual's spiritual field of perception and enables him to benefit from a lucid and extremely joyous consciousness in the other world. The goal of divine spirituality is to make the Source known and to enable human beings to reach perfection, which is achieved through the celestial soul's process of maturation. To undertake this process, it is necessary to adopt the mindset of a student—that is, to always be thirsty for the Truth.[2] Such an attitude avoids reaching for just any kind of spirituality, but one that is divine. If we mention divine spirituality, it is because not every spirituality qualifies as such; at the same time, not every divine spirituality is suitable for a spiritual student. The spirituality that is suitable for a spiritual student is one that develops his thought in the direction of the process of perfection; one that is in line with the times, rational, and capable of being practiced in such way that it can be applied in normal daily life within our familial and social environment; and one that does not contradict the essence of the monotheistic faiths.[3]

To be able to expand our spiritual field of perception, we have to consider spirituality as a science. In general, if we do not analyze any subject through the means relevant to that subject, the doorway that leads us to its application will remain closed, exactly as if the contents of the subject simply did not exist for us. Likewise, if we fail to consider spirituality as a science and do not act upon it through its own specific means, we will have hidden its application from our field of perception and will imagine that such a phenomenon does not even exist. It is clear, therefore, that if we are negligent and intentionally disregard divine spirituality, then like any other science, it will not automatically reveal itself to us. In that case, what will we really be able to do once we enter the spiritual world and leave this one behind?

In summary, to comprehend truths and help expand our spiritual field of perception, we have to consider divine spirituality as a science and practice it with the mindset of a student. If our field of perception expands, we will enter the spiritual world with alertness, lucidity, and joy after leaving this world, and instead of feeling nostalgic we will feel as though we have returned to our original abode.

Who is a Spiritual Student?

Someone who has the aptitude of becoming a spiritual student automatically wants to learn and understand Truth (that which is true and real). A belief in a superior being is concealed within him, and he feels that life has a deeper meaning and he has to do something toward that end. Inwardly, he feels that material life, even the most successful, cannot be the main goal in and of itself, and that death cannot be the end of everything. Such a person naturally observes ethics and innately tends toward justice and fairness. The external and superficial rituals of the religions do not satisfy him, and in some cases he even feels allergic to them, particularly if the performance of these rituals were imposed upon him during childhood. When encountering spiritual truths, he feels a peaceful happiness within. If he unknowingly enters a deviated spiritual path, it will usually be only for a temporary period. As soon as he finds a true spirituality, his heart will become calm, he will feel elated, and he will be transformed into a true spiritual student thirsty for understanding the truth. He feels a positive sense of anxiety about his spiritual destiny. This anxiety, along with his love and enthusiasm for understanding the truth, will become his main inner driving force such that he is constantly working to reach the goal. This natural motivation causes him to remain steadfast in his spiritual conviction about the path he has discovered toward the truth. With the passage of time, signs that are indicative of spiritual maturity will appear within him: an enduring peacefulness settles within the depths of his being; the rigors of life induce less psychological pressure upon him; he enjoys greater peace of mind; his heart is filled with hope for the future; and he does not fear death, for he knows a better life awaits him in the other world.

To protect himself from the harm of potential deviations, a spiritual student should keep the following practical points in mind:

♦ To be aware that he is never alone and that the Source is always beside him in order to help him.

♦ To be aware of his imperious self at every moment.

♦ To observe rights and duties to the extent of his abilities, and to always be ready to help others at all times.

♦ To seek divine satisfaction first and foremost in his decisions, and to use his common sense in doing so.

Observing these points enables a spiritual student to develop his celestial reason and thus acquire a better understanding of material and spiritual life. By doing so, he will become more spiritually mature and acquire better self-knowledge, at which point he will receive the gift of greater divine knowledge. If he succeeds in knowing the Divinity of the Time, he will have entered the "highway," and from then on he can continue his process of spiritual perfection without the danger of deviating and with a sense of certitude, safety, and greater speed until he reaches the ultimate destination.

In summary, a spiritual student is one who is thirsty for the truth, always considers the Source to be present and observant, and tries not to neglect fighting his imperious self for an instant. In his decision-making, he seeks divine satisfaction, and in his social life he always strives—through the observation of rights and duties—to be active and beneficial for society, considering the practice of spirituality as a duty for the maturation of his soul.

40. The Path of Perfection at a Glance

The fundamental principles of the path of perfection can be summarized as follows:

♦ An intelligent, transcendent entity (the Source, Chapter 2).

♦ A few fundamental axioms in spirituality: the divine presence, the principle of causality, and the vital essence (Chapter 2).

♦ The celestial soul's process of growth and maturation (the process of spiritual perfection): every being is endowed with a continuous ascending movement that enables it to arrive at its destination. The destination for human beings is to reach a level of perfect self-consciousness such that they can communicate with all the beings of the universe with complete clarity and alertness and understand all of the existing graces in creation and fully enjoy them. To reach this destination, every being completes the stages of its path of perfection by undertaking the processes of growth and maturation until it returns to its origin (Chapters 3 and 4).

♦ The psychospiritual organism: the reality of a human being is a living, dynamic, and evolving psychospiritual organism consisting of two main components: the celestial soul or "positive pole," which bears the divine breath and endows human beings with the potential to acquire ethical virtues; and the terrestrial soul or "negative pole," which contains the animal instincts and is extraordinarily active. The terrestrial soul also ensures the biological life of the body and serves as the necessary complement to the celestial soul. At the time of birth, these two souls merge with one another and form the "self" or the "total ego." This bipolarity is the *sine qua non* for beginning the process of spiritual development. To reach perfection, we must necessarily travel a thousand spiritual educational stages (the path of perfection) that are analogous to university-level coursework. To accomplish this task, a uniform time limit has been designated for everyone. With hard work and persistence in the right direction, we can reach the destination before the end of this time limit, or we can lose this opportunity as a result of our negligence, allowing the time limit to expire without reaching the destination. Thus, each of us is responsible for his own destiny to the extent of his free will, and must inevitably answer for his actions and intentions.

- ◆ Inner Struggle: the celestial soul, through the "ego," and the terrestrial soul, through the "imperious self," are constantly in a state of fighting against each other. By nature, the celestial soul is drawn to the Source, while the imperious self (the harmful impulsive pressures of the id) pulls us forcefully toward the material pleasures of this world, such as power, wealth, honors, luxuries, lust, etc. We should also not neglect the excesses of the super id (the instinctual impulses of the celestial soul), for it may subject us to rebellions of a mystical nature. Each of these two sources of impulses (the id and the super id) is drawn toward excess, and it is up to the ego to establish equilibrium between them with the help of its willpower and celestial reason.

Accordingly, the basis of our work for reaching perfection is to have attention to the Source and to fight against the imperious self. This requires that at the outset we delve within and search inwardly, know the different components of our being, and recognize the strong and weak points of our personality. Until we enter the realm of action, we will be unable to realize that without help from the Source, we cannot reach inner equilibrium.

Why have we come to earth? Residing in a biological body is similar to a temporary but necessary exile. Life on earth is intended as a university for the education of the celestial soul, and for someone who knows how to benefit from it, it is a goldmine. During this earthly life, we have to acquire sufficient spiritual reserves and knowledge of divine truths to enable us to remain in the interworld and continue our process of perfection there. The opportunities for advancing in this new dimension (the interworld) are unsurpassed, for we can continue our process of perfection there in a state of exhilaration and joy, and advance toward the Source, i.e., divine proximity. Proximity to the Source is to forever exist in absolute freedom, in His total love, and in a state of ineffable bliss, the exhilarating effects of which are renewed every instant and more sublime each time than the last.

APPENDIX

❖ Creation

❖ Ostad Elahi's Universal Prayer

❖ Glossary

Glossary

Absolute Vali – The total manifestation of the essence, thought, and power of the Source.

Blaming Conscience – Also known as the moral conscience and the voice of the conscience, the blaming conscience (superego) is one of the faculties of the celestial soul. Whenever an individual performs or intends to perform an action that is contrary to ethics, the blaming conscience reproaches him.

Body-Milieu – an ensemble consisting of one's present body and psyche, as well as the environment and its effects. "Body" mostly refers to the creational factors that form one's nature and essence and determine a person's psychological, intellectual, and behavioral aptitudes.

Causal – That which exists in the causal world and is subject to causal determinism. According to this definition, anything that originates from the terrestrial part of human beings is causal.

Celestial Reason – Once transcendent reason evolves from an embryonic and immature stage and reaches maturation, it transforms into celestial reason.

Celestial Soul – A soul with a heavenly (celestial) origin that descends to earth to merge with the terrestrial soul and form the "self" or psychospiritual organism of human beings. The celestial soul of human beings bears the divine particle, which endows it with the potential to acquire divine attributes. This soul is also the origin of reason, willpower, moral conscience, and the super id.

Certifying Conscience – One of the faculties of the celestial soul (the superego) that assures human beings their action has been in conformity with divine satisfaction.

Character Unit – The "self" or psychospiritual organism of human beings is composed of numerous character units or "spiritual cells" that constitute their psychospiritual attributes.

Concupiscent Faculty – One of the tools of the terrestrial soul that produces the necessary psychological energy for impulses geared toward desires and pleasures. In excess, this energy leads to hedonism, greed, jealousy, etc., while in deficiency it manifests in the form of depression and a lack of motivation. When this faculty is in equilibrium, it results in modesty, self-restraint, and temperance, ensuring preservation of the self and the species.

Divine Entity – The Source and all the perfect beings that have joined Him.

Divine Particle – A particle that originates from the breath of the divine soul and confers upon human beings the potential to develop divine virtues.

Divine Spirituality – A spirituality established through affirmation by the Source and thus in opposition to spiritualities without the Divine, power-based spiritualities, recreational-based spiritualities, etc.; its fundamental principles are based on the essence of the divine teachings relayed by the monotheistic envoys.

Divinity of the Time – The facet of the Source that manifests in a given era to facilitate the spiritual progress of human beings of that time. Although the Source is unique, His relationship with human beings varies over time in accordance with their intellectual development.

Ego – The origin of reason and the source of thought. Its role is to tend to the inner conflicts and struggles between the commanding impulses of the id, on the one hand, and the prohibitions of the superego, on the other. The formation and development of the ego is gradual, beginning from childhood and taking shape through encounters with the realities of life. Subject to the principle of realism, which leads human beings to evaluate their actions, the ego is not limited to that of one's present life, but rather includes egos from one's past lives as well, which remain in the realm of the unconscious; as such, we call it the Total Ego.

Eternal Worlds (Eternal Spiritual Worlds) – The eternal abode of souls, meaning the abode of those who have reached the end of their time limit for the process of perfection and have undergone the final judgment (evaluation).

Field of Perception – The realm in which thought circulates. This field includes the totality of an individual's perspectives, knowledge, experiences, memories, ideas, imaginations, etc.

Id – The id is situated in the realm of the unconscious. It is the source of biological instincts and impulses, which include vital needs and whimsical terrestrial desires.

Imaginative Faculty – One of the tools of the terrestrial soul that results in the awareness of details. It is the source of imaginations, fantasies, etc., such that it could be considered the intellect of the terrestrial soul. If the energy of this faculty dominates that of the transcendent reason, it will result in trickery, hypocrisy, deception, improbity, reverie, etc.; if the energy of this faculty is deficient, it will lead to a lack of sound judgment, fantasies, naiveté, foolishness, etc. When such energy is combined in equilibrium with the energy of the transcendent reason, however, it will generate meticulousness, skillfulness, ingenuity, tactfulness, prudence, etc.

Imperious Self – The imperious self is the source of whimsical desires, carnal rebellions, and illegitimate and harmful desires of the terrestrial soul (id). If these harmful impulses are not controlled by the ego, they will lead to faults, weak points, and negative thoughts and feelings, driving us in a direction away from inner balance and self-control and thus distancing us from the Source.

Inspiring Conscience – One of the faculties of the celestial soul (the superego), with the help of which human beings receive inspiration as to whether an action is in conformity with or contrary to divine satisfaction.

Irascible Faculty – One of the tools of the terrestrial soul that produces the necessary psychological energy for the fight-or-flight response. In excess, it generates wrath, aggression, hostility, etc., while a deficiency results in lethargy, a lack of zeal, a lack of effort, a lack of self-esteem, etc. In equilibrium, this faculty leads to courage, as a result of which human beings can stand up to transgressions and defend their rights.

Metacausal – That which lies outside the realm of receptivity to causality. According to this definition, anything that originates from the Divine Entity or the celestial part of human beings is metacausal.

Metacausal Energy – Energy coming from the Divine Entity (the Source) or from positive spirits in direct contact with the Source, such as envoys and authentic saints.

Natural Meditation – One of the fundamental principles of natural spirituality. Natural meditation involves having constant attention to the Source in daily life, considering Him present and observant at all times, and seeking His satisfaction in our decisions and actions.

Natural Spirituality – A spirituality with a metacausal origin whose principles are compatible with the natural development of the celestial soul.

Saviors – High-ranking souls of the first order that are the noblest of beings and assigned with divine missions, including revelation and the guidance of all beings.

Self – An entity that comes into existence from the fusion of the terrestrial soul and the celestial soul.

Superego – From the perspective of psychology, the superego is the origin of the moral conscience and is responsible for declaring the goodness or malevolence of an action to the ego. Formed through contact with the family and social environment, the superego is the origin of the voice of one's conscience, the sense of remorse, and the feeling of guilt. The superego is not limited solely to the moral conscience (the blaming conscience), but rather includes two other faculties: the inspiring conscience and the certifying conscience.

Super Id – In contrast to the id, which is the source of biological impulses and whimsical animal desires, the super id is the source of the celestial soul's impulses. The id is subject to the pleasure principle (worldly and animal pleasures), whereas the super id pursues spiritual pleasures. If the super id is controlled by a prudent ego, it will manifest in the form of faith and divine love, and will express itself through a love for spirituality, altruism, etc. The super id is the origin of positive celestial energy, which the ego needs to control the imperious self.

Terrestrial Soul – A soul with a terrestrial origin that bears animalistic characteristics and directly bestows life upon the human body. The terrestrial soul is the culmination of the perfection of mineral, vegetal, and animal spirits that have reached their maturation; it is the origin of animalistic impulses.

The Principle of the Middle Way – The Source has given human beings the faculty of discernment, freedom of choice, willpower, the freedom to act, and guidance. Consequently, each person is responsible for his own destiny to the extent of his reason and free will. When something lies beyond the realm of an individual's free will, his destiny depends upon divine providence. The principle of "the middle way" states that ordinary human beings are subject to neither absolute determinism nor absolute free will, but rather are situated between the two.

The Path (Process) of Spiritual Perfection – A path that all beings must follow until they reach their own perfection. For human beings, this means reaching a level of perfect self-consciousness such that they can communicate with all the beings of the universe with profound insight and complete awareness—that is, to understand all the existent graces in the universe and to enjoy them fully.

Total Ego – Includes the present "self" defined by the science of psychology, as well as all the "selves" from past lives preserved in the realm of the unconscious. Once a human being reaches self-knowledge and divine knowledge, he will understand all the acquisitions of the total self in his self-consciousness.

Total Soul (Quiddity) – The form in which the Source manifests in order to make itself known and comprehensible to the creatures of the entire universe, including human beings.

Transcendent Reason – The reasoning power of the celestial soul that has yet to reach its maturation.

Ultra-Cerebral Memory – The celestial soul's memory, situated in the realm of the unconscious.

Vali – The representative of the Source on earth.

Worker Self – The terrestrial soul in the form of the worker self appears as a responsible and persistent worker that automatically and in accordance with its natural instincts regulates the biological and psychological functions of the body, including nutrition, reproduction, immunity, affections, etc.

Notes

Preface

1 *La Voie de la Perfection* [The Path of Perfection] was first published in 1976 by Seghers Publishers, and was subsequently reprinted three times with minor revisions. The book has thus far been translated and published in English, German, Italian, Greek, and Polish.

2 Ostad Elahi's forename. The title of "Ostad," which literally means "professor" or "master" in Persian, was added posthumously by those who became cognizant of the true nature of his spiritual personality.

3 His last post before retiring was as President of the Court of Appeals for the province of Mazandaran.

4 A collection of Ostad Elahi's oral discourses published in two volumes.

5 To date, seven CD's of Ostad Elahi's mystical music have been released.

Chapter 1: The Meaning of Life

1 As the content of this work originates entirely from the philosophy of my father, Ostad Elahi, I have commenced each chapter with one of his sayings.

2 One of the reasons we consider the psychospiritual organism to be a material entity of immense subtlety is that it is subject to the laws of causality like any other material being. On this topic, see *Spirituality is a Science.*

3 By "natural development of the soul" we mean the development of the celestial soul in accordance with its nature.

4 The adjective "natural" signifies that the nature of the celestial soul, like that of the body, has its own nutritional specificity, just as the nutritional specificity of herbivores, for example, differs from that of carnivores. Therefore, if we want the celestial soul to develop naturally (meaning in accordance with its nature) and to reach its maturation (perfection), we must nourish it with "nutrients" (divine ethical principles) that are suited to its creational nature.

Chapter 2: A Few Basic Axioms

1 An axiom is an initial proposition that is incapable of being proven and whose existence provides the basis upon which a proof or science is based.

2 In other words, images of the Source human beings have created to preserve their own self-interests.

3 Although by definition an infinite chain of causes is not strictly impossible from a logical standpoint, it must nevertheless have a base, even if it is infinite.

Chapter 3: The Process of Perfection

1 In the hierarchical levels of perfection, there exist beings more elementary than minerals that we have called "infratoms," but since they are not well-known at the present time, we will not discuss them further. For a more detailed explanation, refer to *Spirituality is a Science*, Study III.

2 In certain exceptional cases, the soul of a single animal is transformed into a terrestrial soul.

3 Infratoms, particles, atoms, molecules, and increasingly complex structures.

4 Two inferior spirits must combine for the germs of a higher spirit to appear within this fusion. For example, the effects of the mineral spirit must combine with the effects of the vegetal spirit so that as a result of their perfection, the germ of the animal spirit can come into existence.

Chapter 4: The Process of Spiritual Perfection

1 The terrestrial soul has an earthly origin, meaning that it results from the perfection of the mineral, vegetal, and animal spirits.

2 With the exception of certain incorruptible bodies.

Chapter 5: The Self, The Total Ego
(Part I – The Celestial Component)

1 Jo Godefroid, *Les fondements de la psychologie* (Montreal: Vigot, 1993).

2 The imperious self refers to the manifestations of the id's harmful impulses—that is, internal pressures that are illegitimate and harmful as much from a divine and moral standpoint as from a social one. See also Chapter 6.

3 See Chapter 14.

4 Here, we are referring to psychospiritual, non-divine phenomena that have a material goal, such as the occult sciences, etc.

Chapter 6: The Self, The Total Ego
(Part II – The Terrestrial Component)

1 Transcendent reason is the reasoning faculty of the celestial soul.

2 "Worker" is used here in the same sense as in the expression "worker bee."

3 See Chapter 5, note 2.

Chapter 7: Controlling the "Self"

1   A selective osmotic membrane is a living membrane located between two solutions of different concentrations. Transcending simple physicochemical laws, it selects the kind and amount of elements that must pass through it.

Chapter 8: Celestial Reason

1   Every divine principle possesses both a material and a spiritual benefit; otherwise, it is either inauthentic or it has been altered.

2   When human beings first encounter an authentic spirituality, this energy (which is **metacausal**) manifests itself through an attraction toward, or even an inexplicable love for, performing spiritual activities.

3   On the importance of intention, see *Medicine of the Soul*, Study III (Cornwall Books 2001).

Chapter 9: Ascending Succesive Lives

1   A temporary spiritual world located between the material world and the eternal spiritual worlds; see Chapter 10.

2   It should be noted that the principle of ascending successive lives differs considerably from theories based on metempsychosis. See *Spirituality is a Science*, Study V and VI, and *Knowledge of the Soul*, Chapter 8, refuting the notion of metempsychosis.

3   According to the extensive spiritual research of Ostad Elahi, the duration of this period, which is the same for all individuals, is said to be a maximum of 50,000 years. In addition to this time limit on earth, the celestial soul also has a time allotment in the interworld.

4   If we experience even for an instant a taste of life in the other world, then even the most successful life on earth will have no attraction to us, and will appear so unpleasant and sad that we will no longer desire to return to earth. To accept that it is a great privilege to be kept in the other world, it is sufficient to note the numerous accounts of those who have had contact with the spiritual world, including those who have testified about near-death experiences while only having been able to come close to the border of the other world.

5   In more severe cases, it is even possible for an individual's soul to be spiritually connected to that of an animal, plant, or mineral. As the soul is conscious of its imprisoned state in such cases, it experiences a sense of painful humiliation and great suffering.

6   See Chapter 10, note 1.

Chapter 10: The Interworld

1   Material (matter) here is used in the common sense of the word, since the other worlds—with the exception of the Divine Entity, which is metacausal and therefore non-material—are all causal and in a sense matter, only matter that becomes increasingly subtle. On this topic, see *Spirituality is a Science*, Study III.

2   It is a replicate world for the following reason: every being in the material world will appear in the interworld with the same form and quality as it had at the time of death, and the environment it had in the material world for its process of perfection that was cut short will be replicated for it in the interworld for the period of time necessary .... Ostad Elahi, *Ma'refat ol-Rouh* (Knowledge of the Soul), Tehran, 4th ed., 1971, p. 105.

3   Id., pp. 103-105.

4   Id., p. 105.

5   In the material world, the body severely reduces the sensations of the soul, like a thick glove that dulls the tactile sensations of the hand.

6   *Ma'refat ol-Rouh* (Knowledge of the Soul), pp. 80–81.

7   In other words, completing the required number of spiritual academic credits on earth.

8   Education of thought is a process that consists in building or rebuilding the structure of one's thought with bricks of correct ethical and moral principles. During the course of a person's life, it is education of thought that determines his beliefs, decisions, the direction of his behavior, and in general the sum value of his life.

9   Also referred to as "provisions" or "spiritual capital." Spiritual reserves correspond to the sum of acts one has accomplished with the intention of attracting divine satisfaction and performing one's duty. Helping others, abstention, appropriate fasting and ascetic acts, almsgiving, etc., to attract divine satisfaction are among the factors that increase one's spiritual reserves.

10   It is also possible for the soul to be placed in a provisional hell for a specific period of time. For example, a soul in the interworld may be temporarily connected to the soul of a human being that is suffering on earth, or in extreme cases to the soul of an animal, plant, or mineral. As the soul is fully aware of its state during such penalties, it experiences an incomparable state of helplessness.

Chapter 11: Coming Back on Earth

1 Celestial souls are created in clusters and like to be among their own group when they return to life on earth. Similar to blood groups, different groups of souls are more or less compatible with each other.
2 Ostad Elahi, *Borhân ol-Haqq* (Demonstration of the Truth), eighth ed. (Tehran: Jeyhoun, 1995), p. 334.
3 This includes both biological and spiritual heredity.
4 See also Chapter 23, "The Education and Upbringing of Children."
5 The quality of nourishment depends upon the nature of the food and in particular its positive or negative (licit or illicit) origin.
6 To a certain extent, both groups of individuals can usually be recognized from the time of their childhood by observing the relationships they establish with their parents and the environment.
7 The ultra-cerebral memory is a component of the unconscious that is analogous to the hardware of a computer, whereas the cerebral memory of our present life can be likened to its software. As long as we live on earth, these two memories are in constant interaction with one another through the unconscious, even though we are not always aware of such interaction.

Chapter 12: Forgetting our Past Lives

1 This situation is applicable to ordinary souls.

Chapter 13: Death

1 The state of the celestial soul in the body is similar to that of a coil that has been compressed to the maximum extent possible.
2 The presence of individuals with faith at the moment of death and at the burial is beneficial for the deceased.

Chapter 14: The Eternal Worlds

1 It is also possible to reach perfection during one's life on earth before the expiration of the allotted time, or to be granted permission not to return to earth in order to complete the remainder of one's process of perfection in the interworld.
2 In reality, the extent of divine mercy and justice is so great that they nullify the meaning of the word "eternal" with regards to hell (the worlds of ill-being).

3   Just as souls residing in the interworld do not have access to the interworlds of other planets, souls residing in the worlds of well-being (paradise) do not have access to the paradises of other planets. Therefore, in this regard their happiness is relative, for any type of limitation detracts from total happiness.

4   Causal gravitation is exerted on beings living in the material world and in the causal spiritual worlds that are still unable to overcome the effects of the causal gravitational field upon them. As long as a human being is under the influence of causal gravitation, he cannot expect to acquire total freedom. As he gradually draws closer to the Source, however, the pressure of the causal gravitational field over him decreases and his control over it increases. Perfection means having complete control over the field of causal gravitation, which enables a human being to gain access to the world of perfection (the metacausal world). Even at the highest levels of paradise, the pressure of the causal gravitational field still exists. (On this subject, refer to *Spirituality is a Science*, Study III.)

5   In scientific terms, this means that the vibratory frequency of such beings has become aligned with that of the Source.

6   The "end" for beings does not mean "nonexistence," but rather a transformation or evolution, for anything that is created will never return to nothingness.

Chapter 15: Evil

1   The necessary tools for exercising free will are reason and willpower.

2   According to the same story, Azazel was of an inferior level to the angels from a creational standpoint, but lived among them and had even been appointed as the leader of a group of angels.

3   Venomous human beings are the most dangerous thieves of faith. Their words carry a negative effect and can erase faith from the heart of a believer. These individuals appear in different forms in society: they may have no religion, or have some religious aspect to them. If they are religious, they have an extremely presentable appearance, are quite sociable, and carry out their devotional activities according to people's liking. Often, they are unaware of the falsity of their faith, and since they are entangled in the trap of the "divine" stratagem, they consider their own false faith to be the truth, perceiving truth as falsehood and vice versa. The Source has left them to their own devices and has engrained them in their deviated thinking such that they are caught up in the vicious circle of their own actions.

4　The negative forces have no effect over anyone who is in control of his imperious self.

5　Carbon monoxide is a colorless, odorless, and highly toxic gas.

6　The Source as He truly is, and not as He is conceived by intellectual interpretations and dogmatic beliefs.

Chapter 16: Determinism and Free Will

1　A reference to Imam Ali's saying: "Neither determinism nor free will, but the principle of the middle way."

2　The divine will.

3　This is also applicable to beings such as minerals, plants, animals, etc., that are subject to determinism by creation as a result of lacking the faculty of discernment.

4　*The divine system* is the ensemble of causes and means used by the Source for His acts of mercy, justice, and order.

5　If we pay attention to our surroundings, there are many such examples. For instance, someone who has taken everything into account still misses his flight due to traffic congestion, and later learns that the plane he was supposed to travel on was involved in an accident.

6　Pride, which is the substance of arrogance and self-centeredness, results from ignorance of oneself. A proud person is not aware of his own true worth: he considers his own attributes to be more valuable than they are, and the good attributes of others to be less valuable than they are.

7　See Chapter 28.

Chapter 17: Invariable and Variable Destinies

1　The meaning of the word "destiny" is also applicable to a group, a nation, and even to all of humanity.

2　In some of the ancient texts, Moses is rescued by the Pharaoh's wife.

3　See Chapter 11.

4　This applies to astrology as well as all other forms of predictions.

5　See Chapter 31.

Chapter 18: The Recording of our Actions and Thoughts

1　Prayer, helping others, etc.

2　Referred to as benediction in some cultures.

3　See *Spirituality is a Science*, p. 134.

Chapter 19: The Consequences of our Actions

1 This does not mean that every occurrence in life is the "result of an action"—many occurrences such as those stated above are the direct "reaction" to our actions.

2 For someone who is working with the goal of progressing in spirituality, every positive action creates an opportunity for a similar action, but under slightly more difficult conditions. For example, if someone does something out of altruism for an amicable individual, it is possible that a similar opportunity may arise for him, but this time toward someone whom he does not generally like. If he succeeds in performing this second act of altruism as well, then the effects of his first action will be recorded in his being.

Chapter 20: Our Conduct in this World

1 See Chapter 35.

2 When the Source wants to forgive an individual who has transgressed upon the right of another, He compensates the harm suffered by the oppressed out of His own grace in such way that the oppressed gladly and willingly forgives his oppressor.

Chapter 21: Realism and Positive-Seeing

1 See Chapter 24.

2 In jealousy, one wishes for another person to be deprived of some benefit. Such a feeling is a form of malevolence that should be fought against.

Chapter 22: Men and Women

1 The case of certain divine saints who chose to remain celibate is a different matter. These individuals had complete self-control and could marry or not based on their own will or the divine will. For example, Buddha decided to remain celibate after his enlightenment, even though he had previously been married. Christ had no desire to marry and did not receive any order to do so; conversely, other saints with the same rank chose to establish a marital life.

2 For example, the prayer of a united couple has the same effect as that of a congregation.

3   If there are children, their rights should be considered as well.
4   See also Chapter 11, the "creational factors."

Chapter 23: The Education and Upbringing of Children

1   A correct education of thought during adulthood can decrease or even entirely eliminate the negative effects of one's childhood.
2   It is as if an osmotic relationship between the child's psyche and that of the parents has been established from the moment of birth.

Chapter 24: Religion

1   According to the same definition and description by which all of the envoys, saints, and true monotheists have known Him.
2   Observing divine principles is a part of rights and duties.
3   These individuals, whose spiritual rank was not recognized by the public in their own time, were often harassed by the authorities and mostly lived in seclusion and utmost simplicity.
4   As the Persian mystical poet Esfehani said: "For they are all faces and the Truth is He, there is none other than the One that can truly be."
5   The presence of false religions is necessary for the spiritual ecosystem of society. In reality, how can we know the truth without confronting its opposite?

Chapter 26: Miracles

1   It is clear that not everyone can make such requests: usually, they are sought by mystics and ascetics who have been able to acquire some spiritual reserves as a result of their acts of devotion.
2   *The effect of words:* someone whose words carry an effect is endowed with the divine impact, which is evidenced by the fact that everything he says materializes and touches a person's heart.

Chapter 27: The Divine Envoys

1   In cases commonly known as *near-death experiences*, the cord connecting the celestial soul to the body has not yet been severed, even if an individual is considered dead in a clinical sense. The cord is severed when an individual truly dies and the signs of definitive death manifest within him.
2   On the subject of divine argument, see Chapter 9, "The End of the

Allotted Time for Successive Lives."

3   Muhammad's battles were solely defensive in nature, and the territorial expansion of Islam occurred after his death.

4   Bahram for the Zoroastrians, Elijah for the Jews, Jesus Christ for the Christians, Mahdi for the Muslims, etc.

5   See Chapter 28.

Chapter 28: The Spiritual Hierarchy

1   See "Creation" in the Appendix.

2   Among the Saviors, only seven have been known by name. In his manuscript *Unveiling of the Truths*, Ostad Elahi refers to eleven Saviors, but names only the seven who have been recognized in some of the religious texts (archangels).

3   The "divine regard" is a force that is always positive and beneficial, and is the source of both material and spiritual grace. For example, in terms of spirituality, the divine regard can purify a being and elevate his rank, even to the same level as that of the person casting his regard.

4   See also *Foundations of Natural Spirituality*, Study 7.

5   All three have manifested during the course of the past 15 centuries in seven-century intervals.

6   See Chapter 35.

Chapter 29: Prayer and Meditation

1   Divine energy is a *metacausal* energy that transcends causality and encompasses all causes and effects. Someone who prays is able to use the energy he obtains through prayer to benefit others. For example, he can direct the benefits of this energy to an ill person to alleviate his pain or even cure his illness; to a distressed person to relieve his stress; to a deceased person for the blessing of his soul, etc. Although praying for others carries a spiritual reward, we should not insist or make demands in our prayers, but rather it is best to leave the results to the Source.

2   Certain prayers accompanied by music and joyous melodies excite the soul and charge it with exhilarating effects. This form of prayer strongly motivates the soul and is sometimes performed by the adherents and mystics of different religions.

3   See Chapter 25.

4   The heart in this context refers to the seat of deep feelings, inner thoughts, affective excitements, love, etc., related to the centers in our

nervous system responsible for affections and emotions.

5   In other books by the same author, this concept has also been referred to as "attention."

6   Some religions consider certain times during the day and night as more propitious than others for attention and prayer. For example, nighttime (after midnight, preferably from 3 a.m. until dawn), dawn, noon, and dusk.

7   This is a state that Ostad Elahi calls *permanent attention*.

8   Apart from the mistakes and errors that result from human nature. When we reach this state of permanent attention, He automatically helps us in such way that our mistakes are not spiritually detrimental to us. He mitigates our reactions and effaces them through material harms such as minor illness or material losses.

Chapter 30: Music

1   The psychosomatic effects of music are in the process of being re-searched and better understood.

2   There are particles that emanate from the sound of the tanbour and cre-ate scenes. That is why when we pay attention and close our eyes, we can see those scenes as though they were playing on a movie screen. Each song relates to a particular scene (Words of Truth, Vol. II, Saying 356).

3   The quality of our "self" or psychospiritual organism is determined by the extent to which transcendent reason has transformed into celestial reason, as well as the extent to which the super id dominates the id.

4   This intention might manifest itself as a spiritual surge that the artist is not necessarily aware of, or that he may feel but not be able to express.

5   See note 2 above.

Chapter 31: Dreams

1   Psychoanalysis does not recognize the existence of the celestial soul, and postulates that dreams arise solely from the psyche and originate from the unconscious, without having any spiritual meaning or premonitory function. Although the theory of the origin of psychological dreams is correct to an extent, one cannot ignore the numerous reliable accounts that confirm the veracity of genuine premonitory and spiritual dreams.

2   Ordinary consciousness in human beings is the equivalent of active vigilance; this state enables an individual to adapt himself to his environment.

3　Ostad Elahi says: "The other world is like a mirror; each person sees in it his own image."

4　Variable destinies are recorded on the variable tablet; see Chapter 17.

Chapter 32: Communicating with Souls

1　Such souls are not vicious by creation, but since they play a negative role for human beings, they are commonly called "vicious."

Chapter 33: Other Beings

1　It is said the earth's gravity has no effect on such beings, who live in the earth's atmosphere and derive their nourishment from it. Matter is not an obstacle to their vision or movement, and they can displace themselves at a speed close to that of thought.

2　See also Chapter 22.

Chapter 34: Spiritual Pitfalls

1　One should be careful not to confuse this with schizophrenia.

2　Those who enter the spiritual world on their own and without any protection.

3　Gradually, lucrative mystical organizations and movements will replace false guides; though their goals are similar, they may use different methods.

4　Particularly the group of invisible creatures hostile to human beings; see Chapter 33.

Chapter 35: Guidance

1　The "theatrical aspect" of spirituality refers to the display of spiritual powers such as wonders, discoveries, etc.

2　See Chapter 28.

3　"Core" refers to the essence of the great divine religions; see Chapter 39, note 3.

4　Rationality has two stages: transcendent reason, which exists at creation, and celestial reason, which develops as a result of the gradual evolution of transcendent reason.

5　Refer to Chapter 26.

6　The term "Divinity of the Time" can be analogized to a computer password: whoever uses this expression sincerely will receive an answer from the Source, even if he doesn't immediately realize it.

7   One of the clear signs of sincere faith is being worried about one's spiritual destiny or fearing the Source—that is, fearing one's own mistakes and weaknesses when confronting divine tests. A spiritual guide lives in fear and hope: fear of divine tests, and hope that he will have the opportunity to attract divine satisfaction.

Chapter 36: Spiritual Techniques

1   On the relationship between the terrestrial soul and the body, refer to Chapter 6.

2   The goal of mild ascetic practices, such as the customary fasting prescribed in various religions, is not the weakening of the body but rather a form of abstinence that enables human beings to better understand the discomfort of those who are subject to hunger. Furthermore, the duration of such mild ascetic practices is limited, and they are also beneficial for the body.

3   See Chapter 8.

4   Of course, such states only apply to those individuals who are of sound mind and psychologically (mentally) balanced, which is also what distinguishes such experiences from neurotic and psychotic symptoms.

Chapter 37: Fighting Against the Imperious Self

1   The imperious self, which originates from the terrestrial soul, is both a receptor of negative energy and a generator of harmful desires and impulses.

2   See Figure 2 in Chapter 5.

3   Celestial reason: the perfected state of transcendent reason.

4   A sound mind stems from celestial reason.

Chapter 38: Self-Knowledge

1   For example, the Disciples of Christ had felt the manifestation of the Source in Christ, but John the Baptist had reached the level of seeing the exact truth of that manifestation. Likewise, the daughter or wife (depending on the various sources) of the pharaoh had seen the truth of Moses. Khadija, the wife of the prophet Muhammad, had felt the truth of Muhammad, whereas Ali, his cousin and son-in-law, had seen his exact truth. In contrast, individuals whose celestial souls have plunged to the level of darkness feel hostility and even hatred toward great divine saints, like the feeling of Salome's mother toward John the Baptist.

2   We say divine spirituality here to distinguish it from other forms of

spirituality such as those without the Source, mercantile spiritualities, the search for paranormal powers, and so forth.

3   Each component has its own specific tendencies.

4   See also Chapters 5 and 6.

5   The celestial soul is endowed with a genetic inheritance, a part of which is composed of the good and bad attributes it has acquired over the course of its past lives. Genetic inheritance begins to take shape from the moment the celestial soul fuses with the terrestrial soul for the first time, and thereafter evolves with each earthly life. That is why, for example, certain children react better than others to temptations of anti-ethical or anti-divine actions, without having received any specific instruction.

6   According to the science of psychoanalysis, the id is the origin of vital needs, desires, aggressive tendencies, etc.

7   Reminder: the imperious self is the origin of illegitimate and harmful pressures, desires, and impulses of the terrestrial soul or id. If they are not controlled by the ego, it is these same impulses that generate flaws, character weaknesses, bad thoughts, negative tendencies, and negative feelings—in short, all that is generally detrimental to the celestial soul and drives us in the opposite direction from inner equilibrium and self-control.

8   Reminder: in the form of the worker self, the id appears as a responsible and diligent worker that assumes in an instinctive and autonomous manner the physiological and psychological functions of the body (vital needs), such as nutrition, reproduction, immunity, affective states, etc.

9   The id and the super id are in opposition to one another: if either of them is not controlled by the ego, one will inevitably fall into excess and take control of the other.

10   For example, solely to satisfy the desires of the super id, an individual is willing to even endanger his life or abandon his family and society ... and head to the seclusion of nature.

11   With regard to controlling the animal desires of the id, refer to the previous chapter, "Fighting Against the Imperious Self."

12   Metacausal: beyond causality. An example of how metacausal energy governs causal energy can be seen in some of the devotional sessions of certain mystical orders. During these sessions, metacausal energy neutralizes the burning capacity of fire, which is a causal property, to the extent that even objects at the site of the devotional session become

incombustible. Pity this energy is spent on recreation and displays of power rather than the growth and development of the celestial soul.

Chapter 39: The Spiritual Student

1   A severe reduction in one's field of perception may result in a state of "spiritual autism."

2   Truth includes the Source, divine matters, and all that is true and real.

3   Ostad Elahi sets forth the essence of Religion in a few points as follows:

> If the essence of religion is what you seek
> Embrace these basic principles and beliefs
> First, place your faith in the Source
> Who is peerless, unique, and invisible
> Second, consider every being as good
> For none is bad by origin
> Malevolence is borne of the acts that you see
> Strive therefore to avoid such deeds
> As for those who are considered benevolent
> Respect them as they are known to be
> Third, in every time and in every place
> That which the wise deem virtuous
> And engenders order and comfort for all
> Originates from the Source indeed
> Thus practice it toward yourself and others
> And refrain from all that is contrary to it
> Beyond that, whatever creed you may choose
> That does not oppose the principles above
> Is permissible provided that its prescriptions
> Are practiced with conviction too
> [...]

Borhân ol-Haqq (Demonstration of the Truth), eighth ed. (Tehran: Jeyhoun, 1995), p. 306.

Appendix: Creation

1   Written by Ostad Elahi at the age of 29, *The Unveiling of Truths* sets forth the account of creation. This unpublished, handwritten manuscript was on display in 1995 in Paris at an exhibition entitled "The Life and Work of Ostad Elahi." The present account is derived from a few extracts of that work.

2   "Moment" here does not refer to the short unit of time we ordinarily understand it to be.

3   "Infinite" should be considered in its relative sense.

LaVergne, TN USA
17 March 2011
220514LV00003B/20/A